Evaluability Assessment

Evaluation in Education and Human Services series

Editors:

George F. Madaus
Boston College
Chestnut Hill, Massachusetts, U.S.A.

Daniel L. Stufflebeam
Western Michigan University
Kalamazoo, Michigan, U.S.A.

Previously published books in the series:

Evaluability Assessment

A Practical Approach

M. F. Smith

with preface by

George Mayeske

Kluwer Academic Publishers
Boston/Dordrecht/London

Distributors for North America:
Kluwer Academic Publishers
101 Philip Drive
Assinippi Park
Norwell, Massachusetts 02061 USA

Distributors for all other countries:
Kluwer Academic Publishers Group
Distribution Centre
Post Office Box 322
3300 AH Dordrecht, THE NETHERLANDS

Library of Congress Cataloging-in-Publication Data

Smith, M. F.
  Evaluability assessment.

  (Evaluation in education and human services)
  Bibliography: p.
  1. Evaluation research (Social action programs)
I. Title. II. Series.
H62.S586   1989   361.2'072   89-15433
ISBN 0-7923-9036-9

Printed in the United States of America

Contents

CONTENTS

Foreword

My interest in and appreciation for program evaluation began in the early 1970's when conducting a curriculum development research project at the University of Florida's P. K. Yonge Laboratory School. This interest was sparked when it became apparent that testing the success of an education program required more skills than just statistics and research methods. After pursuing additional formal schooling, I embarked on a career featuring educational program evaluation as its central thrust--as a private consultant, later in a university health sciences center involving seven academic colleges, and then in the Cooperative Extension Services of Florida and Maryland. Adding evaluability assessment (EA) to the performance of evaluations, to program development, and to teaching about evaluation has been a significant development for me personally, and I hope to those who have been participants with me in each endeavor.

This book grew out of many of these experiences and involved numerous colleagues who made significant contributions. First among these is Dr. George Mayeske, Program Evaluation Specialist, Extension Service, U. S. Department of Agriculture, Washington, D. C., who (1) initiated the project (which took us to all the case-study sites) with approval for the federal portion of the funds after the two of us had worked together at the University of Florida's Winter Institute on Evaluating Cooperative Extension Programs; (2) teamed with me in site visits to the states where the process was field tested; and (3) listened attentively to my continuous "out loud" thinking and challenged me to dig deeper. Quite often his challenges were in the form of silence, which would force me to question myself. I sometimes thought George already knew everything I was struggling to piece together and was just letting me learn by the discovery method!

I am deeply grateful to George. This book would not have happened without his interest in EA and his initiation of the project on which it is primarily based.

Next, is all the diligent professionals at the fieldtest sites who were willing to risk with us on a project in which--at the beginning--we could not explain exactly what had to be done or what was in it for them. I am still amazed that they took on the tasks and worked so hard. Their efforts, their reactions, and their constant challenges of the "theory" furthered the process development. Some of the people who come to mind most readily are Dr. Charley Clark, Program Evaluation Specialist in Cooperative Extension and leader of the EA project in Illinois, who contributed beyond what was required to get that case study completed and the report written. Charley became interested in the process as well as the Illinois product. He contributed unselfishly of his time and his ideas both through the Illinois EA and later in a six-month sabbatical with me at Maryland.

Dr. Doris Smith, Assistant Director of Cooperative Extension, University of California, was the impetus for the selection of the second EA implemented in this project and contributed mightily to its success. Dr. Dennis Pittenger at UC Riverside, and Dr. James Grieshop at UC Davis made sure all the tasks were performed and that the CA master gardener EA stayed on schedule, and wrote the final report. Their insight about the process and their diligence in getting it completed are appreciated.

So many others contributed that it is impossible to mention each one's special effort, e.g., Dr. Don Steinbach, Project Supervisor, Wildlife and Fisheries, Texas Agricultural Extension Service, Texas A&M University, and all the others involved in the aquaculture study; Dr. Lynda Harriman, Assistant Director, Oklahoma Cooperative Extension Service, Stillwater, and all the Resource Management faculty who participated in the home-based business EA; the three county faculty in Maryland who worked through the 4-H study: Robert Shirley, Carroll County; Ava Baker, Baltimore County; and Hope Jackson, Howard County.

Special appreciation is extended to Dr. Dick Weismiller, Department of Agronomy; Dr. Nan Booth, Community Resource Development; Dr. Bill Magette, Department of Agricultural Engineering; Ms. Ruth Miller, Home Economics Agent in Calvert County, and Mr. Reg Traband, Agricultural Agent in Harford County, all at the University of Maryland, and Dr. Margaret Ordonez, formerly Department of Home Economics, University of Maryland, now at the University of Rhode Island. These six individuals and I carried out the water resources EA. Without any reservation, they have been the best team with which I have ever worked. They trusted me and each other, worked hard--often doing tasks to which they were not at first committed--and have since become spokespersons for the product we produced and the EA process.

Dr. Craig Oliver, Director of Maryland Cooperative Extension Service and Associate Vice Chancellor for Agricultural Affairs, University of Maryland System, has been supportive of the two EAs done in Maryland (4-H youth and water programs) AND supportive of my time spent in developing the process both here and in the other four states. I could not have proceeded without this support.

Dr. Michael Quinn Patton, author of many books on evaluation, Past President of the American Evaluation Association, and Leader of Extension programs in the Caribbean for the University of Minnesota, critiqued a previous draft of this book. His suggestions were very helpful.

Dr. Leonard Rutman, Partner in the Price Waterhouse Management Consultants firm in Canada and author of many books on evaluation--one on evaluability assessment--provided the last review. He made many constructive and very useful comments.

This book is much better because of Rutman's and Patton's reviews. I appreciate their help and their encouragement to proceed was reassuring.

I am also grateful to my students who provide an always changing source of stimulation. Greg Corman fits in this category plus he assisted with the layout of most of the models in this book.

Lastly, I wish to thank my husband, Dr. Wayne Smith, Director of the Center for Biomass Energy Systems at the University of Florida, Gainesville. He has contributed to me in so many ways--always supportive of my professional and personal interests.

M. F. "Midge" SMITH
University of Maryland
College Park, MD
1988

Preface

Upon my return to the U. S. Department of Agriculture (USDA) after a thirteen year interlude conducting educational evaluations in the former U.S. Department of Health, Education and Welfare (DHEW), I was handed a Congressional mandate for a study of a nutrition education program oriented to the needs of low-income families. It was soon apparent that the study was commissioned out of a conflict between the Senate and House Appropriations Committees. It was a prime candidate for a cut by the former and for the maintenance of funding by the latter. Realizing that this was a very narrow tightrope for an evaluator to walk, I wondered if there might be others in the nutrition community besides the Appropriations staffs, who would have a more balanced view of the program. It was then I recalled a series of Evaluability Assessments (EA's) with their "stakeholder" interviews that my former colleague at DHEW, Joe Wholey had been initiating. Modeling our efforts after his, my colleagues and I interviewed some sixty-seven individuals who had some viewpoint about or interest in the program. The effect of interviewing these "stakeholders" and responding to their interests through a periodic newsletter created a broad constituency for the study and took it out of the narrow confines of the Appropriations Committees. When the 1980 election results caused some of the Committee members and their staffs to lose their positions of influence, there was still broad support for continuing the study.

Feeling very buoyed up by this experience I began preaching the virtues of EA to my Extension colleagues. I was quickly reminded by them that that particular nutrition education program was a "top-down" program which was carried out in much the same way everywhere. Most of Extension programming on the other hand, started at the "grass-roots" level with programs designed to meet the needs of local citizens. It was true that some guidance was given to the "grass-roots" by the State and Federal partners but that the flow of planning was for the most part upward. Here then was a challenge--could EA be adapted to the results of a planning process which is the near opposite of the conditions under which it was first developed? And if so, what would the products look like and how and to whom might they be useful?

Dr. Midge Smith of the University of Florida and I had already begun to collaborate on some EA work as a part of Florida's Annual Winter Evaluation Institute. In response to a request by me for support, the Federal partner (Extension Service, USDA) was kind enough to make special funds available to test the adaptability of EA. With the kind permission of her superiors at the University of Florida and later at the University of Maryland, we embarked upon a voyage with Midge at the helm. The details of that trip are dealt with in the body of this report. However, for the trip to begin some careful revisions had to be made in Joe Wholey's (1979) maps and routes as was the case also with those who followed him.

The first condition that confronted us was that there were very limited funds available to carry out the project. There were nowhere near enough funds to put a team of observers in the field to interview local agents and to see how a program was being carried out. But then again it didn't really make much sense to do that anyhow. Many agents spend only a part of their total time on any one program and even for those who do, their activities are often very seasonal in nature. Hence, it would not be a good investment of resources to field a team for these purposes. On the other hand we could pull together in a central location, a number of local agents who themselves carry out the program and impact directly on clientele, if their State would cover their travel costs. This proved to be a feasible solution which has profound implications for the way EA's are conducted in Extension. Under such conditions the evaluator becomes the facilitator of a group process wherein the members of the group work cooperatively through a series of steps to develop a number of products. No one is threatened by the evaluator since s/he is merely facilitating the process. No group members are appalled by the evaluator's lack of program content expertise since s/he is not expected to have such. There may be differences of opinion and viewpoint among the group members but these are not seen as being provoked by the evaluator. We have called this a staff centered approach to EA and Midge expands on it nicely in subsequent pages.

For four of the trial cases reported in this work, the facilitators were Midge and myself--third party evaluators from outside the local state organizations. We did not bring any preconceived notions about the program to the EA--such would not have been possible since we often knew little if anything about the program nor did the local EA team know much, if anything about us. The fact that we were new, from out-of-state with the sanction of the Federal partner provided some impetus for them to attend to the process. (This is not meant to downplay the great importance of the State's sanction and commitment of time and money.) We are not sure yet how the process will work when/if the EA is conducted totally with in-house personnel. Other considerations will come into play. Our experience to date suggests that a third party to the program from within the State (preferably an evaluation staff representative) may have greater success as a facilitator than would someone directly from the program being studied. This is so because it is easier for them to keep the process moving and on target if they have not been party to the administrative decisions, details and functions of the program. Indeed, a "state-of-ignorance" often is sufficient justification for detailed probes by the facilitator--probes which might otherwise be threatening or frustrating to the workgroup but which can help to bring out unstated assumptions, etc.

This staff-centered approach tends also to produce a consensus among the workgroup members. In the course of the EA process they often reconcile differences that they may have or recognize improvements that can be made in the program and may even put them into effect before completion of the EA. This was considered a desirable development because busy local agents and State staff rarely have much time to spend in planning together. As a result however, we have not had conflicting program models that needed to be reconciled at the end of an EA.

Where should EA go from here if it is to be a viable tool for Extension programming and evaluation? In addition to the trial cases described in this book other EA's have now been completed successfully, e.g., Family Well-Being in Delaware, Home-Based Businesses in Alabama, 4-H in Mississippi and Pennsylvania, Marketing of Fresh Produce in Guam, 4-H Middle Management in Hawaii, Economic Development in Kansas, Leadership Development in Washington, etc. However, for EA to really become useful in Extension, mechanisms need to be fostered to first, institutionalize such skills and later, support and reinforce them. EA skills are not something an uninitiated person can take directly from a workshop and apply. Rather, the development of EA facilitator skills needs careful and direct nurturing through the close working together in actual situations, of those more experienced with those less experienced. When a sufficient critical mass of such collaborative efforts has been attained then the other supporting and reinforcing mechanisms such as networking, workshops, training sessions, and symposia can be brought in to play. Perhaps the Federal partner will be generous enough to assist with the support of these next steps in the process, too.

GEORGE W. MAYESKE
Program Evaluation Specialist
Program Development, Evaluation
and Management Systems
Extension Service
U.S. Department of Agriculture

March, 1988

Evaluability Assessment

CHAPTER ONE

Introduction

Evaluability assessment is a diagnostic and prescriptive tool for improving programs and making evaluations more useful. It is a systematic process for describing the structure of a program (i.e., the objectives, logic, activities, and indicators of successful performance); and for analyzing the plausibility and feasibility for achieving objectives, their suitability for indepth evaluation, and their acceptability to program managers, policymakers, and program operators. This is accomplished by:

o clarifying program intent from the points of view of key actors in and around the program;
o exploring program reality to clarify plausibility of program objectives and the feasibility of program performance; and
o identifying opportunities to improve program performance (Wholey, 1987).

Evaluability assessment began in the early 1970's by Joseph Wholey and his associates at the Urban Institute in Washington, D. C. (Nay and Kay, 1982; Wholey, 1979). Since its inception, the process itself and one of its key components --stakeholder involvement in evaluations--have been continuously in the literature, e.g., Dunn, et al., 1981; Eichelberger, 1986; Freeman and Solomon, 1981; Greene, 1987;

Lawrence and Cook, 1982; McCorcle, 1984; Nay and Kay, 1982; Patton, 1984; Rog, 1985; Russ-Eft, 1986; Rutman,, 1980, 1983, 1984; Wholey, 1979, 1981, 1983, 1987. Though these efforts have been important in heightening interest in the process, they have not contributed sufficiently to a science of methodology. Attention has been heavily focused on program management and on the agencies sponsoring the studies and only lightly on implementation procedures (Freeman and Solomon, 1981; Lawrence and Cook, 1982); techniques have been scarcely defined (Holloway, 1981)--Schmidt et al. (1979) being an exception--with few guidelines for replicability.

Rog (1985) attempted to study evaluability assessments (EAs) conducted in or sponsored by the different agencies from 1972 to 1984. Her searches led her to conclude that the process had not permeated departments beyond Health and Human Services (HHS--formerly the Department of Health, Education, and Welfare, DHEW) and Education, and that the number conducted per year dropped dramatically after Joe Wholey left HHS. (Wholey was the Deputy Assistant Secretary for Planning and Evaluation at DHEW.) She attributed this pattern of diffusion and decline in use to Wholey's advocacy for the method--while he and the other associates who conceived the process were active in its implementation, its use increased; when they became less active, its use declined.

However, the scarcity of concrete defined methodology may have had as much or more to do with the minimal adoption of EA as the advocacy of its creators. In other words, a process may need to meet the same implementation requirements as a program if it is to be successful. In this case that would mean clearly defined outcomes for an EA and clearly defined and plausible activities (methods, steps, tasks) for reaching those outcomes.

In 1984, a project was initiated to define the evaluability assessment process in a practical methodological sense and to encourage adoption in the Cooperative Extension Service. The development process was advanced by implementing six EA's with five State Cooperative Extension Services and the United States Department of Agriculture (USDA), Extension Service (ES), cooperating. Implementation proceeded iteratively, one after the other, each in a different major programming area and in five different states: Illinois, California, Maryland, Texas, and Oklahoma. The programs studied were for elected officials, master gardeners, 4-H youth, aquaculture producers, and home-based business owners, respectively, for the five states, plus the sixth study was conducted in Maryland on the water quality/quantity program. After each iteration, procedures were analyzed and revised to clarify, and where possible, to simplify to make the process more usable and more "operator robust." In the interim, a number of other EAs have been successfully implemented, using guidelines included in this text.

Evaluability assessment was originally conceived as a way to improve impact evaluations and that was the impetus for this cooperative project with ES/USDA. Impact evaluations began receiving great emphasis in the Cooperative Extension Service (CES) with the FY84-87 reporting period (Smith and Straughn, 1983). However, during the first two studies in Illinois and California, it became apparent to all involved that EA could be a powerful tool for program improvement both before and after implementation--first as a process for planning a plausible program and second as a way of examining an existing program to determine plausibility. Thus, two of the last three studies had program improvement as their only focus: the Texas aquaculture program EA was intended to review the present program and identify changes to make it more effective and to ensure that activities were plausible for a slightly different goal statement; the Oklahoma home-based-business program was almost entirely future focused. That program was just beginning; program goals were still in process of being clarified and only one major client activity had taken place. The final study, on Maryland's water quality/quantity program, began as the traditional prestep to an impact evaluation but quickly grew into a program development mode.

Evaluability assessment is a comprehensive and complex undertaking. Factors that influence it include characteristics of the process itself, the organizational context in which the EA is performed, and structural and process features of its conduct. All of these are further influenced by the values of participants and stakeholders and the need to address the interests of potential users of findings. Given a level of complexity of this magnitude, Rossini et al. (1981) suggest that "it would not be sensible to try to distill the relevant knowledge into any simple 'how-to-do-it' rules" (p. 374), yet that is exactly what has been attempted in this text. Guidance has come from questions which seem relevant for a person embarking on any new task, such as:

o What is it? What are its components?

o Why do it? What are its expected outcomes?

o How does it start? What is a logical first step, second step, etc.?

o How did someone else do it?

Thus, a set of interrelated strategic steps are defined to communicate interpretations of evaluability assessment theory as postulated by others and to describe practical and useful applications growing out of the experience of implementing the process in six different settings.

DEFINITION OF TERMS

Brief definitions are presented below for a number of the terms and concepts used in this book. Some readers will be quick to point out that these meanings do not capture the complex nature of the entities they represent and they will be right! However, the definitions are offered to provide a common conceptual framework from which shared under-standings can emerge about the process called evaluability assessment.

A program is a set of planned activities directed toward bringing about specified change(s) in an identified and identifiable audience.

Evaluation is the process of ascertaining the decision areas of concern, selecting appropriate information, and collecting and analyzing that information to report data useful to decision makers in selecting among alternatives (Burry, 1973).

Program evaluation is evaluation of a program (combining the first two definitions, above) for the purpose of determining its operations and/or effects (intended or unintended), relative to the objectives it set out to reach, to contribute to decision making surrounding the program.

Summative, impact, and effectiveness program evaluations all gather data on the results of programs. All three determine to what extent a program does or did what it intended to do; summative and impact evaluations may focus on intended and unintended effects whereas effectiveness evaluations are concerned with intended results.

Formative, process, and implementation program evaluations all focus on the ongoing program to determine what about it is working and what is not, and whether it is being carried out as intended, so that changes can be made to increase its probability of success.

Impact vs. improvement. Patton (1986) differentiates the two as follows: "Improvement involves a judgment about whether or not something is better, whereas impact involves the more limited question of whether or not something is different. An observed difference may or may not constitute improvement, depending on who is making the value judgment about whether the change is for better or worse" (p. 70). Impacts can be observed, improvements cannot.

Evaluation design is a plan for providing information to answer specific questions to achieve defined purposes for identified stakeholders or, said differently, a plan for collecting and interpreting specific data to answer identified questions for defined purposes.

Program theory is a means-ends hierarchy, a cause-effect linkage of program activities with outcomes, a representation of what happens in a program to lead to its outcomes.

Components/Elements are key parts of a program, with defined objective(s), activities, resources, and indicators of success, causally linked to overall program goals.

A stakeholder is a person/group of people with a vested interest--a stake--in a program and/or evaluation. Stakeholders are affected by and can affect the program and/or evaluation in important ways. One can be a stakeholder to a program without also being a stakeholder to an evaluation of that program.

Resources are any and all inputs necessary to successfully implement the activities of a program, e.g., staff, time, materials, money, equipment, facilities.

Performance indicators are descriptions of what can be observed that will signal achievement of activities, objectives, and goals.

Evaluability is a judgement about the feasibility of measuring achievement of a program and/or its parts--its end goals and/or intermediate objectives, i.e., Is the program properly structured? Are performance indicators defined? Will they measure what is intended? Are sources available and sufficient to provide the necessary information?

Plausibility is a judgment about the extent to which necessary and sufficient conditions exist for a program to succeed, i.e., Are activities and resources of the right type and amount to bring about the desired change? (The desired change, typically in the form of objectives and goals, must be clearly defined to make this determination.) If the program is ongoing, then plausibility requires activities to be implemented in sufficient amount and quality.

ORGANIZATION OF REMAINING CHAPTERS AND APPENDICES

Ensuing sections are arranged as follows: Chapter Two includes an overview of the evaluability process with background on its evolution, from a pre-intensive-evaluation step to being an evaluation in its own right. Benefits are described which accrue to the program staff, the program, and the organization as a result of achieving the two primary outcomes: definition of a program's theory and identification of stakeholder interest in a program. Ten tasks are identified for implementing evaluability assessment from determination of purpose and securing commitment to planning for specific utilization of results. These tasks represent more separate steps than others have reported (e.g., Jung and Schubert, 1983; Rog, 1985; Wholey, 1979) with the intent of clarifying and simplifying the process as much as possible.

Chapter Three describes the first series of steps in an EA: determine purpose of the EA (formative, summative, planning), secure commitment from the key stakeholder(s), and identify program staff and/or other individuals to implement remaining tasks. The role of the work group is defined and team characteristics and dynamics are described: personal commitment, number of members, characteristics of members, stability of membership, style of leadership, and the building of trust.

Chapter Four presents procedures for defining program boundaries, i.e., for setting limits on activities to be included in the program to be studied, and identifies some of the forces which set a program in place. In Chapter Five, general guidelines are described for identifying and analyzing program documents.

Chapter Six explains procedure for identifying/ developing the theory of a program. The concept of "theory" used here is an identification of the structural and operational characteristics of a particular program--not the global, conceptual schema of social scientists. Program theory and causality is discussed along with similarities of theory development and model specification. Different formats for models are described with examples provided of logic and functional parts from the Cooperative Extension EAs. Guidelines are offered for how many models to construct, who should define program theory, defining the theory, and validating the model with staff experience.

In Chapter Seven, stakeholders are defined as persons or groups who impact a program in very significant ways and/or who are similarly affected by actions of the program. A rationale is presented for their input to an EA; methods are described for their identification and for prioritizing the list when resources will not permit all to be interviewed. Guidelines are offered for preparing interview questions, for selecting interviewers, and for conducting interviews to insure useful data.

Chapter Eight discusses formal steps for analyzing and summarizing stakeholder interviews. Guidelines are offered for data handling and processing, reducing, and displaying data. Examples from the CES EAs describe specific microsteps for analysis where the number of interviews is small and where the number is large. Summary verification is also described.

Chapter Nine describes the major questions around which stakeholder needs, concerns, and differences should be examined: agreement on overall intent of the program, about who is to be served by the program, about support activities and resources, and future informational/evaluation requirements.

In Chapter Ten, determining plausibility of the program theory model is discussed. Conditions are identified for an assessment of plausibility with criteria for clearly defined goals, and clearly defined components/activities. Nine questions are offered to help determine sufficiency of components/activities, and three for adequacy of resources. Suggestions are made for taking some of the judgment out of the plausibility call: have staff identify their assumptions about the problem-solving process participants must go through to achieve program goals and what will motivate the participants to want to go through the process. Examples are presented from one of the CES studies.

Chapter Eleven is about drawing conclusions and making recommendations, the *piece de resistance* of an evaluation. Several questions are explored: who should draw conclusions and make recommendations, what they are made about, and how they can be justified. Within the last question, the types of data generated in an EA--mostly qualitative and primarily perceptual in nature--are described and potential biasing threats discussed. Validity concerns are addressed in the language of the quantitative question asker even though it is clearly noted that such concerns are understood differently by naturalistic evaluators.

Utilization of results is discussed in Chapter Twelve. This process occurs throughout the previous steps. However, when all the tasks are completed and the final conclusions and recommendations are made, decision makers may choose from five alternative courses of action:

1. Decide to evaluate the program (or some parts),
2. Decide to change the program (or plan),
3. Decide to take no further action,

4. Decide to stop the program,
5. Do not decide, ignore the EA.

Each course of action is discussed with suggestions for implementation when/if it does occur.

Chapter Thirteen contains a reflection on the process and the implementation experience; philosophical and methodological issues are discussed.

Appendix One is a brief description of the Cooperative Extension Service, the agency in which was implemented the evaluability assessments used as case studies in this book.

Appendices Two, Three, and Four are excerpts from the reports of three evaluability assessments implemented in state Cooperative Extension Services. Appendix Two, which contains excerpts from the report of the statewide 4-H youth program in Maryland, is the most formal of the three. That EA was conducted subsequent to the other two after procedure had become better clarified, thus that report follows more closely the steps as described in this book. Included in the 4-H excerpts are the executive summary, the description of procedure, the section which discusses the evidence and presents the basis for conclusions, the summary conclusions and recommendations, and an addendum with the complete program model (logic model plus activities, resources, and performance indicators). The full report had the following sections not available here due to space limitations: titles of each stakeholder interviewed, questions asked of each stakeholder group, and the complete summary of stakeholder interviews.

Appendix Three includes excerpts from the report of the Illinois local government officials program. Procedures for major steps are described: bounding the program, selecting planning committee members, data collection, and model development. Potential limitations of the procedures are also identified. Findings are discussed relative to plausibility of impact, measurability of impact indicators. and stakeholder desire for program information. Changes in and about the program which occurred after the EA was completed are described, e.g., the Kellogg Foundation granted additional funding, the University put one of the program's soft-monied employees on a "hard" line, etc. The logic model for the program is included in an addendum.

Appendix Four has excerpts from the report of the California master gardener program. Circumstances leading up to the EA are described and then the process followed in the EA is discussed on a meeting-by-meeting time frame, e.g., at the April 10-11, 1985, meeting of the California work team and the two outside "consultants," the procedures manual was reviewed, stakeholders were identified and a schedule established for conducting the interviews, interview questions were developed, and a set of tasks were identified and assigned to work team members for completion prior to the next session scheduled for July, 1985. The report continues in this manner through the final meeting in October, 1985, when the EA had been completed, where conclusions were drawn and next steps planned. The program logic model is included in an addendum.

CHAPTER TWO

Evaluability Assessment: Overview of Process

DEFINITION

Evaluability assessment (EA) began as a process for analyzing a program's structure to determine the extent to which it was suitable for effectiveness evaluation (Wholey, 1979); later its potential for determining the extent to which a program was capable of being managed for successful results was recognized (Wholey, 1983); and this CES effort has demonstrated its contribution to developing programs capable of achieving intended outcomes and capable of providing evidence of that achievement.

EA is a method for examining a program (or a proposed program) to assess its structure, to determine plausibility of the program achieving intended goals, the evaluability of those goals, and the utility of implementing further evaluation of the program.

o   A proposed program is plausible if it has clearly identified goals and effects, a logical set of well-defined activities or components, and the necessary resources to implement the activities/ components.

o   A program, itself, is plausible if, in addition, its activities/components have been implemented in sufficient amount and quality to bring about intended change.
o   A program (or a plan) is evaluable if criteria and procedures for measuring achievement of intended goals have been identified which can be feasibly implemented.
o   An evaluation has utility if the program is evaluable and there are well-defined uses for information about the program.

Judgments about plausibility, evaluability, and evaluation utility are not offered in a vacuum, i.e., a successful evaluability assessment will identify parts of a program or plan lacking on these criteria and suggest ameliorative strategies.

The process may be used (1) as a summative tool--as a preliminary step to an impact or effectiveness evaluation to determine what parts of a program are evaluable and what parts warrant evaluation based on stakeholder interest, and/or (2) as a formative tool--as a way of deciding what needs changing about a program to make it more effective and/or efficient, and/or (3) as a planning tool--as a way to define program goals and to identify plausible activities for achieving those goals and the resources necessary to implement those activities in sufficient quantity and quality.

The planning function of EA may be proactive or reactive, i.e., a program design may be developed to meet plausibility and evaluability criteria or an already developed design may be judged against those criteria. Williams (1976) pointed out how obvious it is to expect that policymakers at the time of choice would have reasonable estimates of the organizational capacity to carry out alternative proposals. "But however obvious that may be, few people have ever thought in terms of analyzing implementation during the decision-making stages" (p. 270).

HISTORICAL PERSPECTIVE

Program evaluation is a process for examining a program to assess its operations and/or effects (intended or unintended), relative to the objectives it set out to reach. Decision areas of concern are ascertained, data are collected and analyzed and put in a form useful to decision makers in selecting among alternatives. There are several types of program evaluation. One type--sometimes referred to as formative--is conducted while a program is ongoing; its purpose is for program improvement. A second type--sometimes referred to as summative--is conducted after a program is stable and expected to have achieved intended effects; its purpose is to gather data on the results of a program.

Evaluability assessment originated in the early 1970's as a way to improve the second type--summative program evaluations. Such evaluations, then and now, were often perceived by policy makers as expensive wastes of time which produced little in the way of timely, useful information. Evaluators, on the other hand, often found programs with grandiose goals and few concrete objectives. This led them to produce evaluations which angered policy makers by highlighting program deficiencies or else the evaluations were as muddled and vague as the programs.

Wholey and his associates decided that an impasse had developed between stakeholders of programs and evaluators of those programs because of differences between "rhetoric and reality" (Nay and Kay, 1982). They explored ways of bringing program rhetoric (i.e., claims about a program) and reality together through a series of quick evaluations (Nay et al., 1973; Scanlon et al., 1971; Scanlon et al., 1972; Vogt et al., 1973; White et al., 1974). These efforts shared several common elements (Jung and Schubert, 1983):

o   Effort to reduce barriers between evaluators and evaluation users by having both involved in shaping the evaluation agenda;

o   Effort to avoid the "goal trap" by early analyses to check for gaps between rhetorical and actual program objectives;

o   Effort to reduce the probability of collecting data on effects of programs with implementation flaws by checking for discrepancies between intended and actual program operations;

o   Effort to prevent resources being wasted on collecting data on "unmeasurable" or unimportant objectives by early determinations of which were measurable and which were most important; and

o   When called for, effort to improve programs and make them more plausible and evaluable by identification of practical management options.

Evaluability assessment is the first of three steps that Wholey (1979) argued should be performed sequentially before implementation of large-scale, resource-intensive impact studies. If the EA showed preliminary evidence that the program could and was functioning as intended, then short-term rapid feedback evaluations based on readily available information should be implemented, followed by performance monitoring to secure evidence that the program was achieving intermediate objectives.

Most discussions on EA still focus on the process as a highly desirable prestep to outcome evaluations, to establish the probability that the subsequent study will be useful (Russ-Eft, 1986; Rutman, 1980, 1983, 1984; Schubert, 1982; Wholey, 1979). However, the process has grown into an evaluation tool in its own right--as a way for determining stakeholder awareness and interest in a program and for determining what needs to be done in a program to make it likely to produce results. It has also evolved into a program development tool--as a way to plan a plausible, evaluable program and to determine resource requirements and availability.

EXPECTED OUTCOMES

Two primary outcomes are expected from an EA:

1. **Definition of a program's theory,** i.e., underlying logic (cause and effect relationships) and functional aspects (activities and resources) with indications of types of evidence (performance indicators) for determining when planned activities are implemented and when intended and unintended outcomes are achieved.

2. **Identification of stakeholder awareness of and interest in a program,** i.e., their perceptions of what a program is meant to accomplish, their concerns/worries about a program's progress toward goal attainment, their perceptions of adequacy of program resources, and their interests in or needs for evaluative information on a program.

When an impact evaluation is anticipated, both of these outcomes should be attained before the evaluation is designed. When a program is being planned or when improvement is the intent, Outcome 1, only, may to be pursued, i.e., having a defined program framework increases the likelihood of program staff managing their programs to achieve intended impacts-- whether or not the impacts are to be measured.

When the purpose of the EA is as a prestep to further evaluation, these outcomes permit a clear indication of whether an intensive evaluation is warranted, and if so, what components/activities in the program can provide the most desirable data. In essence, they prevent evaluators from committing two types of error (Scanlon et al., 1979):

o **Measuring something that does not exist, and**

o **Measuring something that is of no interest to management and policy makers.**

The first type of error exists when the program has <u>not</u> been implemented or when the program is <u>not</u> implemented as intended or when there is no testable relationship between the program activity carried out and the program objectives being measured. The second type occurs when the evaluator brings back information that policymakers and management have no need for or cannot act upon.

Both types of error are avoidable: the first, by defining the program and describing the extent of implementation; the second, by asking stakeholders what they consider important about the program and/or evaluation.

Benefits from Outcome 1, Clarification of Program Theory

Evaluability assessment assists in doing a number of things well but the most important of these is the explication of program theory.* A good program theory describes how a program is supposed to work (Bickman, 1987a), systematically delineates cause-and-effect relationships (Conrad and Miller, 1987; Scheirer, 1987), and as such, provides the rationale for a program intervention. The six EAs used as the primary experience for this book showed the process to be useful not only in identifying the theory of an ongoing program (looking backward) but also in developing theory for the future (looking forward)--not only for looking at what a program is but what one could be.

Theory as used in this context is what Shadish (1987) would describe as microtheory which

describes the structural and operational characteristics of what is being evaluated in enough detail to provide information on the general nature of the project or program, its functioning, and...its changeable component parts (p. 93).

as contrasted with macrotheory which

details the social, psychological, political, organizational, and economic factors that facilitate or constrain change within and outside programs (p. 93).

---

*Chapter Six presents a detailed description of program theory and its role in EA.

Every program has a theory (Bickman, 1987a). For someone to justify the mandate and resources for implementing activities, something is expected to result--either for self and/or for others. Sometimes the expectations are clear but more often than not, they are implicit and/or incomplete and/or unconscious to program staff. Sometimes the lack of clarity is due to insufficient knowledge about an area, sometimes to programs being developed and implemented by individuals who, though highly competent in a technical area like animal or human nutrition, may have no training in social science rationale and methodology, and sometimes to planning being treated as a task separate from implementation.

Some programs may have more than one underlying theory, depending on the set of explanatory variables used in their descriptions (Bickman, 1987a). This is not too surprising since the social problems that many programs are designed to correct are complex with multiple causes and multiple potential solutions.

Defining program theory in this fashion encourages program experimentation and thus problem amelioration with the end result of contributing to our repertoire of empirically based scientific theories of behavioral and social change. Other functions are served by making program theory explicit. Some of these benefit evaluators by making their efforts more successful and some benefit policy makers, but most accrue directly to program staff and clients who are intended beneficiaries of the programs. Examples of these positive outcomes follow.

Increases the Effectiveness and Efficiency of Program Staff and thus the Program's Probability of Success

Information and conceptual gaps may be revealed when delineating the underlying assumptions in a program's theory of action. When these gaps are filled and staff are clear about intended outcomes and the strategies to accomplish them, they are much more likely to be effective. The logically described program provides a basis for proactive decision making and action. As an example, after finishing an EA in California, Pittenger and Grieshop (1985) concluded:

> Although a decision has been made not to conduct an evaluation, understanding of the Master Gardener program has been immeasurably improved--its ambiguities, its strengths, and its weaknesses are now much more visible. It is now quite clear (where) additional time and effort must be addressed ...(p. 8).

Priorities are also easier to determine and to pursue, as noted by a program leader (French, 1985, personal communication) after development of a model of the small farms program in Florida. He commented that for the first time since the program began, he could decide to do an activity or to not follow up on a request and feel like he could defend such decisions based on what these would contribute to program goals.

Results in Immediate Implementation of Program Improvement Actions

In the usual evaluation, recommendations are left to the end, sometimes presented in preliminary presentation of findings but often reserved until the final report is written. Staff may or may not be involved in defining those recommendations and the recommendations may or may not be acted upon.

In contrast, staff of the different programs in the CES evaluability assessments made changes in their programs almost as rapidly as observations of needed changes were discovered and corrective actions conceived. In fact, these actions made it nearly impossible to describe the "present state of affairs" when developing the program models. For example, the staff of the California master gardener program insisted that their model show a different goal than they had been operating under and identified supporting elements (activities, resources, and indicators) to make that goal plausible; the Illinois public officials program staff insisted that activities they were not doing but which they could do be added to strengthen key components in their logic model and that no evaluation take place until these could be implemented.

Jung and Schubert (1983) found the same phenomenon with the eight EAs conducted by the American Institutes for Research between 1980 and 1983; and our reaction to these on-the-spot changes was the same as theirs: It was a heady and satisfying experience!

Helps Distinguish Between Program Failure and Evaluation Failure and Between Theory Failure and Implementation Failure

Programs may be shown as failures as a result of theory failure (implementing activities which have no or the wrong effect on a problem), implementation failure (carrying out activities ineffectively or not at all), or evaluation failure (using a faulty set of assessment procedures). Evaluations also may not succeed as a result of theory failure and/or implementation failure. Theory failure would result from evaluations designed separate from a consideration of the theoretical underpinnings of the programs they were meant to assess (e.g., assessing effects not plausibly linked to program activities) and implementation failure, from not carrying out the required evaluation tasks and/or not carrying them out properly.

So-called black-box evaluations which focus only on outcomes are examples of evaluations which lack the program theory base. They may successfully show that certain effects have or have not occurred but lacking information on the actual nature of the program being evaluated, decision makers cannot determine if failure was inadequate theory and/or inadequate implementation, and if success is found, they will not know how to replicate that success on a larger scale. Patton (1986) described examples of both situations. The first is of a program deemed a failure and terminated, even though it was never implemented:

A program was established by a state legislature to teach welfare recipients the basic rudiments of parenting and household management. The state welfare department was charged with conducting workshops, distributing brochures, showing films, and training caseworkers on how low-income people could better manage their meager resources and become better parents. ...The evaluators interviewed a sample of welfare recipients before the program began... Eighteen months later, the same welfare recipients were interviewed a second time. The results showed no measurable change. ... In brief, the program was found to be ineffective. ...

(The question of why the program was ineffective)... could not be answered by the evaluation as conducted because it focused entirely on measuring the attainment of program outcomes; ... As it turned out, there is a very good reason why the program was ineffective. ...the program quickly became embroiled in the politics of urban welfare. ... the program was delayed and further delayed. Procrastination being the better part of valor, no parenting brochures were ever printed; no household management films were ever shown; no workshops were held; and no caseworkers were ever trained. ...In short, the program was never implemented... (pp. 124-125).

The second is of a program deemed a success and expanded but which later failed because policymakers acted without information about program operations and without an understanding of the success causal factors:

...a number of drug addiction treatment programs in a county were evaluated, collecting nothing but outcomes data on rates of readdiction for treated patients. All programs had relatively mediocre success rates, except one program that had 100% success for two years. The county board immediately voted to triple the budget of that program. Within a year, the readdiction rates for that program had fallen to the same mediocre level as other programs. By enlarging the program based on outcomes data, the county board had eliminated the key elements in the program's success--its small size and dedicated staff. The highly successful program had been a six-patient halfway house with one primary staff counselor who ate, slept, and lived that program. He established such a close relationship with each addict that he knew exactly how to keep each one straight. When the program was enlarged, he became administrator of three houses and lost personal contact with the clients. The successful program became only mediocre. (Patton, 1986, p. 128)

Explication of program theory is the first step for distinguishing among these types of failure, since implementation failure is indistinguishable from theory failure unless there is evidence that the program was implemented with fidelity (Bickman, 1987a), and also since a sensitive evaluation design cannot be developed without having means related to ends.

Permits Estimates of Success of Longterm Programs

Other writers (e.g., Bickman, 1987a; Chen and Rossi, 1983) refer to this function as specifying intervening variables. It allows one to evaluate portions of a program that are expected to lead to other portions. More importantly, though, it requires those intervening variables to be identified and adequately managed. For example, a youth program like scouts cannot be judged as plausible nor can it be shown to be effective if the model contains a large gap between club activities (means) and effective leaders of tomorrow (ultimate outcome).

Increases the Probability of Successful Replication of a Program

Placement of a program into a different environment usually requires an adjustment to administrative and political constraints of different policymakers, thus it is important to know the essential and nonessential components for program success (Chen and Rossi, 1983). Essential components may include not only specific program activities but also other related exogenous factors and intervening processes. Only essential elements should be contained in a program model.

Improves Policymakers' Choices

This function is nearly the same as described above, but is different in terms of policymaker intent. Sometimes it is not a question of whether another environment is similar enough for a proposed program to work but whether other desired activities can continue at the same time. For example, having a defined model of the California master gardener program lead some policymakers to decide against implementing the program because they could quickly comprehend the requirement for resources and see that implementing it would risk failing on some others.

Increases/Improves Staff's Program Development Skills

Staff learn a way of designing a defensible program in a logical fashion to ensure probability of success. The program leader for the Texas EA reported a positive and very observable difference in the programming skills of the EA team when they later met in a departmental meeting which included others who had not participated in the EA work. The California Assistant Director said she learned a definite and definable procedure for program development. Team members of the Maryland water program said the most important outcome from the EA was their learning a process for thinking through and planning a program.

**Benefits from Both Outcomes--Definition of Program
Theory and Stakeholder Involvement**

Increases the Clarity of Options for Evaluation Focus

The original purpose of EA focused on improving evaluations. Delineation of the program's theory of action assists primary stakeholders in making explicit their assumptions about the linkages of means and ends such that evaluation can focus on the linkages where information is most needed at that particular point in the life of the program (Patton, 1986). When the program theory is clearly defined in a time and causal sequence, it is possible to decide that certain parts should be studied before others and some should be examined with more intensity than others. For example, if a certain set of activities is critical to some later component of a program, it would make no sense to collect data on the effectiveness of the later component until it had been determined that the causal activities had been implemented. A clear program theory should make the order of events for evaluation implementation as obvious as the order of implementation of program activities and components.

The second primary outcome, stakeholder awareness and interest in the program, also contributes mightily to decisions about selecting from among the option(s) for evaluation focus. Regardless of what could be evaluated, a purpose of EA is to determine what is important to be evaluated--to determine who wants to know what and for what purpose.

Increases the Organization's Visibility and Accountability

It is often difficult for agencies to assume credit for program impacts for lack of true control groups. Virtually everyone in a small community (and in some not so small) may have been exposed to different amounts of program service. For some programs it may be possible to stratify participants and nonparticipants by level of service. And, in some, one may even be able to attach service delivery dollar costs to each of the service levels--thereby permitting estimates of the marginal cost effectiveness of each service level. However, this may be very difficult for other programs.

Where control groups are not valid and program stratification is not possible, the "hypothesis trail" which links program efforts to program outcomes becomes strong evidence of program impact. If activities are plausible and can be shown to have been properly implemented, some credit can be assumed for any results, plus the linkage of efforts to outcomes should allow assessment of individual outcome costs.

Outcome 2, stakeholder involvement, can generate publicity and credibility for a program and its agency. People take interest in a program when they are asked their opinions about it. They may feel more important as a result of being interviewed and see the program as more important. Greene (1987b) identified this outcome as major for stakeholder evaluations she performed and two report writers of CES evaluability assessments listed program visibility among stakeholders as primary benefits (Clark, 1986; Nelson, 1987).

Encourages Increased/Continued Resource Support for Programs

Wholey (1986) suggested for those interested in maintaining or expanding support for public programs, that three key leadership functions must be accomplished to achieve and demonstrate high performance:

o   Get policy and management agreements on, and commitments to, ambitious but realistic definitions of "performance" for their organizations and programs--in particular, agreements on the outcomes to be achieved and agreements on quantitative or qualitative measures of the outcomes to be achieved.

o   Stimulate high organizational/program performance.

o   Credibly communicate the value of the organization's activities, within and outside the organization. (p. 11)

Evaluability assessment can be helpful on all three. The process calls for program staff to identify realistic definitions of performance by tying activities and resources to outcomes, identifying plausible outcomes, and identifying indicators of performance for key activities and outcomes. Performance is stimulated by increased effectiveness and efficiency brought about by staff having identified effort that contributes to goal attainment and that which is superfluous, and by increased staff pride resulting from having a concretely conceptualized "program" to communicate to important stakeholders. Communication of the value of organization activities, is stimulated by the identification of specific program activities, and by increasing stakeholders' awareness during the interviewing for the EA and the reporting of results.

Increases Staff Interest in and Skills for Conducting Evaluation

Staff are involved in all aspects of the EA, from setting boundaries for the program of interest, to deciding plausibility and evaluability. To make these assessments, they must understand the appropriate criteria and know what is important. They are part owners of the program and any ensuing evaluation. The Illinois EA leader felt that asking staff what they actually are doing before planning an evaluation takes "some of the scare" out of the process.

Increases Staff Pride

A model of program theory provides a concrete description which shows what staff are doing and what they are trying to accomplish, and simplifies that communication. In an EA conducted in Delaware, Nelson (1987, p. 10) reported: "Completion of the logic model has produced a new, more unified confidence that the program is headed in a sensible direction. As one agent said, 'We do know what we're doing.'" Greene (1987b) quoted a staff member of a stakeholder-based program evaluation as saying that "hearing others say good things about the program gave me a boost."

Increases Administration Comprehension of the Program

Staff get the "ear" of administration--their leaders are called on for input on expectations about the program and later involved in reconciling differences in expectations.

Staff Have Time to Think About Their Programs

Program staff have the luxury of spending time thinking about and clarifying their program--for reflecting on goals and strategies for success--away from the usual pressures of day-to-day work. As a result, programs take on new dimensions and staff become more committed to achieving outcomes.

. . . . .

EA's are much like Marshall McLuhan's (1964) characterization of media, i.e., the process is the product. Whether or not impact studies follow EAs, programs will be different and so will program staff as a result of going through the identifying and reconciling steps of the process.

IMPLEMENTATION STEPS

Evaluability assessment may be used as a way to plan defensible programs capable of achieving intended objectives and capable of providing evidence of that achievement, or as a preliminary step to an impact evaluation to determine what parts of a program are evaluable and what parts warrant evaluation based on stakeholder interest, and/or as a way of deciding what needs changing about a program to make it more effective and/or efficient. The process is the same for each of these uses and the same as for any other evaluation effort--data are gathered, comparisons are made, and conclusions are drawn. The number of steps to accomplish this process may differ among individuals, e.g., in 1979, Wholey described EA as an eight-step process; in 1983, Jung and Schubert identified six discrete steps for EAs conducted by the American Institute for Research; and in 1985, Rog found six tasks to be common to most of 57 EAs performed in HHS and Education. Most (47) of the EAs reviewed by Rog were conducted in what was formerly the Department of Health, Education, and Welfare (where Wholey was formerly a Deputy Assistant Secretary) and included all the major tasks identified by Wholey in 1979. The tasks reported by Rog (1985) were:

1. Studying the program's design or the intended program,
2. Studying the program as implemented,
3. Studying the measurement and information system,
4. Conducting an analysis of the plausibility of the program's goals,
5. Preparing various models of the program, and
6. Determining the uses of any subsequent evaluation information.

The methods typically used for gathering information in the 57 studies were:

1. Review and analysis of program documents;
2. Interviews with program staff, policymakers, and project staff; and
3. Site visits to local projects.

Examination of the program as implemented was carried out with less frequency than the other tasks along with the related data-gathering methods of interviewing local project staff and observing the local program.

Ten separate tasks evolved in the EAs conducted in CES (Figure 2-1):

1. Determine Purpose, Secure Commitment, and Identify Work Group Members
2. Define Boundaries of Program to be Studied
3. Identify and Analyze Program Documents

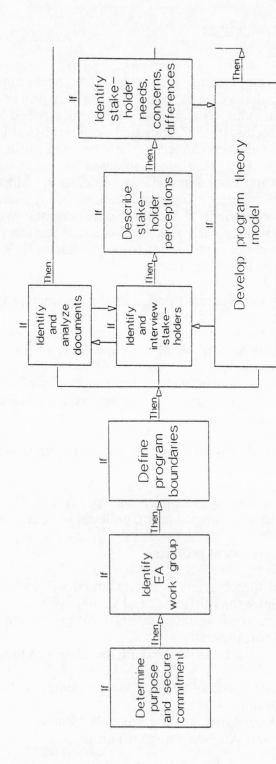

Figure 2-1. Logic Model of Evaluability Assessment Process.

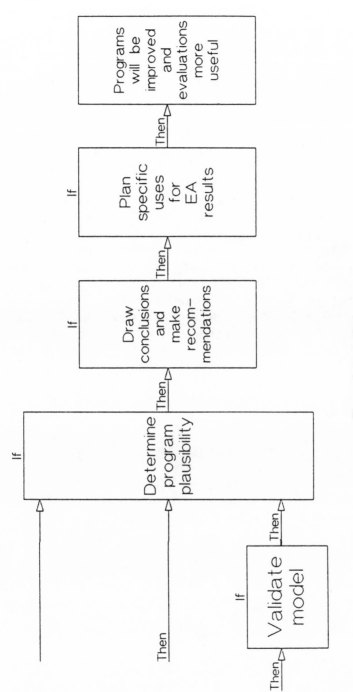

Figure 2-1. Continued.

4. Develop/Clarify Program Theory
5. Identify and Interview Stakeholders
6. Describe Stakeholder Perceptions of Program
7. Identify Stakeholder Needs, Concerns, and Differences in Perceptions
8. Determine Plausibility of Program Model
9. Draw Conclusions and Make Recommendations
10. Plan Specific Steps for Utilization of EA Data.

Each of these tasks is discussed in detail in upcoming chapters with examples from the CES studies and where available, from other agencies. These tasks are presented in a linear fashion but it should be understood that much of the process unfolds interdependently (Figure 2-1). For example, clarifying program theory (Task 4) may suggest a broadening or lessening of program boundaries (Task 2). The EA implementor should become acquainted with all the different tasks and then organize personnel and other resources to get the job done.

CHAPTER THREE

Determine Purpose, Secure Commitment, and Identify Work Group Members

The key players in an EA are (1) the stakeholder(s) for whom the EA is performed, (2) high level program administrator(s), who may or may not be the EA primary stakeholder(s), and (3) the EA work team. The work team is made up of program implementation staff and other task-specific aides.

Once it has been determined that an evaluability assessment may be needed, a meeting should be held with the primary stakeholder(s) of the EA. The goals for this meeting are to (1) explain the EA process, (2) clarify purpose(s) of the EA, (3) receive administrative support for the EA to be implemented, and (4) identify other persons to have input and/or to implement the tasks. Other information may be sought at this initial session but is not mandatory at this time, e.g., identification of other key stakeholders and important written documents that may have influenced their perceptions of the program under review.

As with other evaluative efforts, a half-done study is worse than no study because valuable resources will have been wasted. Thus, high level commitment to the EA is absolutely essential for program staff to devote the time and energy to see it through. The person seeking commitment should describe the three ways that EAs may be used, i.e., for planning a new program, for improving an existing program, or for increasing the utility of an intensive effectiveness evaluation. These purposes along with more specific potential outcomes should be described in terms that clarify the potential impact on the organization where the program is or will be implemented. These should be balanced with an honest appraisal of how long the process will take and anticipated costs in staff time and other resources.

Once the process has been explained, purpose decided, and the administrator is committed to the process, the next step is to identify persons who can help with getting the job done. For example, who should be involved in identifying other stakeholders to be interviewed? Who should help develop the program theory model? Who can (should) conduct and write up interviews? Who will review stakeholder interviews and search for differences in perspectives about the program? Who will decide what differences in perspective are important? Who will decide what the follow-up steps will be after data are collected and reported?

Not all these questions have to be fully answered at this first session. At a minimum though should be the naming of persons who will identify other stakeholders and who will assume responsibility for seeing that tasks are implemented.

For example, at this initial meeting, the Assistant Director for the 4-H Program in Maryland identified a task team to suggest names of key stakeholders, to review stakeholder interviews, and to identify differences in perspectives. He also identified the state 4-H curriculum committee as the group to be responsible for making input to the staff's definition of the program. He left it up to the committee to decide if they did the work or arranged for others to get it done. And, most important, he agreed to communicate to these persons an urgency to commit themselves to the project.

In both the Texas and Oklahoma projects, administrator commitment was secured via long distance telephone exchanges between the program leader and the Maryland-based EA project director. In Texas, nine individuals were identified from different areas and levels of the program to define program theory and one to serve as local liaison.

ROLE OF THE EA TASK TEAM

The task team is absolutely critical to the success of the EA. They should be included at every turn in the planning and execution of the study. Giving them an active role in the decision making will engender vital ownership of the EA and any change it may suggest (McCorcle, 1984). It may mean surrendering a bit of control over the shape of the EA (and/or the program!) but it vastly increases the likelihood that the EA will be completed and that it will yield significant results.

The team participates actively in identifying stakeholders, localizing the interview questions, defining the initial version of the program model, analyzing stakeholder interviews, drawing conclusions and making recommendations, making plans for utilization of results, and deciding how best to disseminate findings to constituencies to further the utilization process.

TEAM CHARACTERISTICS AND DYNAMICS

Factors internal to the core team itself affect success. These include personal commitment to the EA, number of members, characteristics of individual members, stability of membership, style of leadership, and building of trust. An external factor which affects success is organizational commitment. Each of these factors are defined below and followed by descriptions of actual practices which are thought to have aided or thwarted success of the CES EAs.

Commitment to the EA

Commitment by the program team to the EA is just as, if not more, important than commitment from the administrators(s). Team members should be given opportunity to "buy in" to the process before any further steps are taken in implementing the EA. Strategies for securing commitment are (1) say up front, and mean it, that it is okay for any person in the group to decide NOT to proceed; (2) thoroughly describe the process and all the work and time involved for the team; (3) describe outcomes in terms of what team members on other EAs have said they got from participating in the experience; and (4) give each person a chance to identify one or more personal benefits expected to result from being involved in the process.

These steps cannot be rushed. In each of the CES studies, a minimum of three hours was necessary for members to ask questions about the process and talk about potential outcome. Jung and Schubert (1983) found, and we did, too, that the initial structured effort to fully explain the EA process later paid dividends in staff willingness to do the hard work of examining their program's goals, activities, and logic. Trust and openness are absolutely essential. Staff must know that it is okay to opt out if they do not have time or cannot see personal benefits and they must trust enough to identify personally meaningful goals.

Personal goals can be written on a large sheet of paper and taped on the wall at each team meeting. Plans should be made to achieve these and progress noted the same as for the expected EA process products.

Number of Members

In general, the optimum size for an intensive, interactive, task-focused group is 7-9 members (Taylor, 1975). Fewer members are usually insufficient for integration of ideas and more may cause the discussion to become amorphous and the group to segment.

Characteristics of Individual Members

Ideally, core teams should be composed of individuals from as broad a range of levels and types of the program as is appropriate without enlarging the team unnecessarily. A sufficient breadth should be achieved to secure a comprehensive view of program reality. As indicated earlier, members should be favorably disposed to working on such an assignment and comfortable working in the "give and take" of team situations (Rossini et al., 1981).

Stability of Membership

Turnover in team membership and absences have negative effect, particularly on study bounding and program theory development. Some of this cannot be eliminated but the best arrangement is to make team responsibilities known at the beginning so a too-busy or less-committed individual can opt out then rather than later retarding team progress.

Style of Leadership

The team leader needs to operate democratically, at all times supportive of team members and encouraging their participation in all aspects of decision making, but still maintaining authority to ensure that decisions are made and tasks are completed. In a study of success factors in technology assessments, Rossini et al. (1981) concluded that a democratic leadership style was a most important causal factor in performing a well integrated assessment. An "all-channel" pattern of communication between and among leader and team members was also found significant in leadership style of successful technology assessments.

Building of Trust

Some initial trust is necessary to get personal commitment, as described earlier, but it is a continuing goal of team activity. It takes time for team members to learn what each other is like, to risk putting their biases on the table, before real progress can be made. A period of time is needed for such a "shakedown" of attitudes and modes of behavior (Petrie, 1976). Trust is developed in two kinds of group settings: work settings which allow a joint exploration of task-related ideas, concepts, and interests; and informal social settings which allow a wider acquaintanceship to develop (Taylor, 1975).

Organizational Commitment

Participants need to be rewarded for the intensive work and long hours that are required to carry out an EA. This reward comes from administrative support and from peer recognition. Administrative support may take the form of additional resources, released time, encouragement, and administrator participation on the team. Such administrative support will also encourage peer recognition.

OBSERVATIONS FROM THE CES STUDIES

In each case study, team membership was different in terms of number of people involved but in each instance, all levels of the program were included--county staff, state staff, and administration. The amount of participation by the administrators differed and is believed to have significantly affected the ownership and utilization of the EA results. In California, Illinois, and Oklahoma, an Assistant Director for Extension was involved in every meeting of the team. They understood the rationale for EA tasks and were at a high enough level to make immediate decisions about implementation. Consequently, any ideas for changes that were supported by data were discussed and immediately made a part of the program models--rather than waiting until the end of the studies. This made for "messier" studies, in terms of obvious EA impact, e.g., clear before-and-after versions of the logic model, but also made the process more beneficial to the program staff. In the Maryland 4-H study, the Assistant Director participated in two sessions--the first where verbal and written commitment were secured for the EA, and the last where the conclusions and recommendations were presented. Of the EAs which reviewed ongoing programs, the youth study was the most extensive, involved the most stakeholders, had the most data, yielded the clearest and the most significant recommendations--and utilization is pending.

Another key person in all the case studies was a state-level staff member with evaluation expertise. In Illinois and Maryland this person served as team leader and in California, as active team participant. This person was instrumental in seeing that the EA got conducted in an appropriate manner. There are almost always choices in procedure, and decisions need to be made on the basis of getting the most credible results for the precision of anticipated decisions within available resources. Local knowledge and commitment are important in getting these decisions made on a timely basis.

CHAPTER FOUR

Define Boundaries of Program to be Studied

To set boundaries is to define the limits within which one will operate. In this case, it is to define where the program starts and stops. Boundaries can be defined by geographical area, goals, services or benefits provided, clients served, or a combination of these. Some bounding will have occurred prior to the identification of a work team and the process may not be completed in one meeting. A rough recipe is to allow the team an initial period to "wallow" on the subject being assessed, then set the general scope and bounds, and stay prepared for developments which could force change in the study's scope (Rossini et al., 1981). Defining boundaries requires some understanding of the concept "program" and the forces which set it in place.

WHAT IS A PROGRAM?

The concept of a program is fundamentally a question of perspective as seen by policy makers and/or implementors. A key criterion is that there are resources and activities directed toward and presumed to be adequate for the accomplishment of one or more purposes. And, in the most optimum situation, according to Schmidt et al. (1979), some one person has line authority over the resources needed to achieve the end purpose(s).

The nature of a program will differ depending on whether a macro- or local perspective is taken (Scheirer, 1987). The macroperspective is top down and may be simply a funding mechanism to support a certain type of activity. The local perspective may include a specific set of activities prescribed for a specific goal or need.

A program can be narrowly or broadly defined in terms of the functions it performs, the subject matter it covers and/or the geographical areas and/or the population characteristics of those it is designed to serve. For example, a federal- or state-level program may have a regulatory function, a research function, a technical assistance component, and/or an educational thrust. The water program in Maryland has all of these: The Maryland Department of Agriculture has some of the regulatory responsibility, the University of Maryland Agricultural Experiment Station has the majority of the research responsibility, and the University of Maryland Cooperative Extension Service has responsibility for the educational thrust and provides some technical assistance.

Part of the difficulty in defining boundaries is that resources for some programs may not be assigned on a specific program basis. For example, in the California CES program (and likely in other states), one county does not receive a certain number of dollars to implement a master gardener program. Instead, dollars are assigned to broad program areas, e.g., to all programs in a county or to all agricultural programs in that county. The situation may be similar for programs in education. At a university laboratory school, for example, the faculty made the decision to implement the British open classroom concept but funds were not assigned specifically to that program nor was record-keeping separate for outlay of resources. In these situations, it is generally possible to allocate costs to the program sufficiently to appreciate its level of resources use, but it does decrease the clarity of program boundaries.

A second difficulty which may actually be a part of the first, just described, is when individual personnel are involved with several "programs." They have the freedom (responsibility) to keep their time and the other few resources they control in some kind of fluid, dynamic, spread across those different programs. What happens in one area of responsibility influences directly or indirectly what happens in the other areas, i.e., an act or expenditure of resources in one area affects what happens in another area both by the impact of the act and by what it prevented from taking place in the other area. Resources are finite; what is spent in one area prevents expenditures in another.

One way to determine boundaries is to define program goals and then include all activities and efforts which contribute to these goals. That seems easy enough but is fraught with difficulty; goals may be buried so deep in rhetoric that even program staff have difficulty in describing and/or admitting to their true focus. For example, the expectation for a CES 4-H youth program may be stated as "teach leadership (or some other type) skills." Rhetoric aside, the objective for a given county might really be to "win state championships." If that is the case, the true boundaries of the program would include all the activities relating to winning rather than just those on learning "leadership" or "citizenship." The latter becomes process rather than outcomes. In a manpower program the espoused goal may be to improve the employment situations of clients when the true purpose may be to reduce the number on welfare; in a youth neighborhood program, the espoused goal may be to increase youth employment but all the effort may be on eliminating street crime.

Another problem is that the different levels of an organization may often have different goals for the same programs and/or different levels of priority for the same goal or activity. This is not surprising for government programs since they "operate in complex political environments, pushed and pulled in many directions by legislative bodies and by a multitude of funding and regulatory organizations, grantees, and interest groups" (Nay and Kay, 1982, p. 15). For example, the master gardener program as seen by the individual agent at the county level may be primarily a way to get relief from answering telephone calls; from the elected county official perspective, it may be seen as a mechanism for public service, for keeping citizens happy by answering their individual requests; but, from the state or national perspective when rationale for funding is required, the emphasis may be on solving individual client problems.

The conclusion here is that there is no one definition for the boundaries of a program. Where the limits are set on what is to be studied should be based on two factors--importance of the program and decisions to be affected. Since the resources to implement an EA can be significant--at least in staff time-- a "major" program should be its focus. A major program has a substantial amount of resources directed toward an important problem or need. Boyle (1981) defines a major program by virtue of what it is not:

> A major program is not an isolated workshop, event, or course. It is not a single activity. It is not a variety of different educational offerings available cafeteria style. It is not individualized response to the continuous and urgent request from individuals for information. (p.14)

> In short, the lives of people cannot be bettered overnight nor can they be significantly changed in a two hour meeting or a half-day institute. ...A major program needs time and...intensive efforts... (p. 184).

The second factor for setting boundaries is the nature and importance of decisions to be affected. Sometimes it is helpful if the person requesting the study answers the question: "What would you like to be able to say if all the results were in?" This will give clues as to how broadly or narrowly the program is to be defined at the start of the study. The boundaries may change as the other steps in the EA process are completed, especially the identification of key stakeholders' expectations for the program and for the evaluation.

As an example, a program directed toward cleaning up a natural resource like water or air may have several audiences to which activities are directed, e.g., agricultural producers, land developers, industrial plant operators, municipal leaders, residents, and public (agency and elected) officials. The goals and activities for these different audiences may overlap but most likely are not all the same--except in their ultimate outcome, e.g., increasing the quantity of water of satisfactory quality. Another part of the boundary difficulty is that all the audiences to which activities are directed may be either serious contributors to the problem and/or important sources for its solution. In the Maryland water quality/quantity EA, the boundary question was not completely decided until some of the program theory was defined. Discussion of the conceptual framework--in terms of problem cause--and the functional aspects, especially a realistic look at available resources, lead to the conclusion that all the audiences were not equally important as contributing sources of the water problem nor could all of them plausibly be tackled at once from a resource standpoint.

CHAPTER FIVE

Identify and Analyze
Program Documents

Access to program documents should be negotiated early in the EA process, perhaps when the initial commitment for the study is secured. Document review can serve a number of purposes in an EA. Documents can provide clues about program intent and documentation of program reality. They can provide information about the program that cannot be observed because of prior occurrence and because they reflect aspects of the organization that may not be realized in actual program performance (Patton, 1980). They can also suggest areas of concern where stakeholder input may be desirable. Because of the latter function, it is suggested that the review of documents start before stakeholder interviews.

Detailed instructions on document analysis is outside the purview of this book. Included here are recommendations for actions considered critical to the success of the EA effort.

Document analysis may be superior to interviews for collecting some kinds of retrospective data. "A quote taken from an internal memorandum is not subject to the evaluator's bias as are interviewing and observational data" (Caulley, 1983, p. 20). Documents are also nonreactive. This does not avoid errors in reporting but it does avoid bias that can occur, for example, when persons are aware of being under study. On the negative side, documents can be very misleading. Memoranda of all kinds are written with very political intentions (Patton, 1987). What is said is done so with a clear sense of internal politics and must be understood in that context. In addition, the purpose of the document and the organizational position of the person writing it must be understood, if valid observations are to be made.

Examples of documents suggested for review by Wholey (1979) are authorizing legislation, congressional hearings, debates, and committee reports; regulations and guidelines; research, evaluation, and audit reports; program memoranda; speeches; documents describing agency organization and staffing; grant applications and reports from the field.

One way to identify printed documents is to follow the flow of information (paper) through an organization. For example, in Extension, the flow of paper goes downward for gross or general expectations for a program, e.g., legislative mandates, congressional reports, federal and state program guidelines, budgets, annual reports, administrative audits and program reviews, speeches by program administrators, and administrative memoranda. The flow is upward for what the program is doing and for what is needed, e.g., county and state plans of work, reports of accomplishments, management information reports, etc. And, the flow may be both ways or horizontal for information on specific program research and situation analysis. This multidirectional flow for a typical program in CES is shown in Figure 5-1.

Other sources are publicity brochures, press releases, journal articles, and proposals for outside funding. Also, when stakeholders are interviewed, they may reveal documents that influenced their thinking about a program.

At the start of the EA, documents should be read to get a general feel for the intent of a program. Notes should be made of mission statements, goals, audience(s) served, etc. Later on, documents may be secured and analyzed to answer specific questions. For example, in the Maryland 4-H EA, the latest version of the Department's <u>Program Direction</u> document was read prior to interviewing the state staff. The document was analyzed later to make comparisons of its goal statements with those made by county and state faculty and with those included in a national futures-focused document.

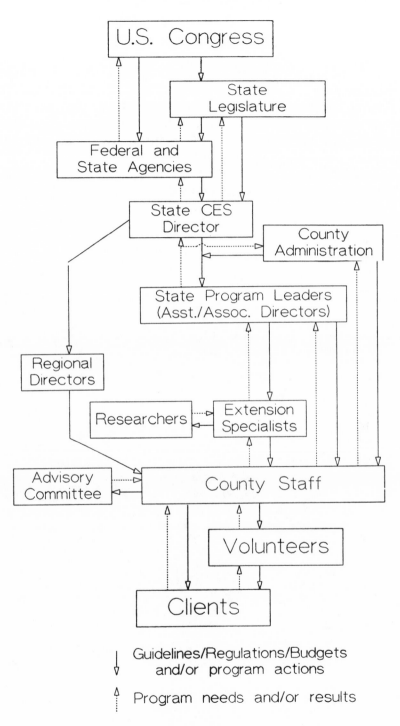

Figure 5-1.

Documents should be read with care. Conflicting documentary statements on what is intended and what is being accomplished may point to confusion among program personnel who read and those who produce these documents. Two other suggestions are: (1) Note the purpose of each document; publicity handouts may contain mostly rhetoric whereas internal materials probably deal more with reality, albeit political; (2) Identify quoted notes so that documents can be referenced and located later.

CHAPTER SIX

Develop/Clarify
Program Theory

The suggested methodology for explaining the theory of a program is simple, straight-forward, and practical. The intent is to identify the assumptions on which program staff act to achieve program goals, i.e., how a program is supposed to work and why, and to identify any gaps in means-ends connections.

PROGRAM THEORY AND CAUSALITY

The questions asked to clarify program theory are questions about what program staff believe affects expected program outcomes, i.e., in what ways do activities, events, and other forces cause or effect changes in the target population? These are means-ends, cause-effect relationships, as they perceive them. Causality in any absolute sense cannot be established because programs contain a variety of components, resources, and procedures which come together in as many ways as there are people who run them and clients who are served by them. However, some reasonable estimation of the likelihood of certain actions bringing about other actions or effects are necessary if one is to understand and try to prove or improve a program's course of action. Evaluation will not lead to final statements about causal linkages, but can reduce uncertainty about such linkages (Patton, 1986).

Cause and effect relationships require a temporal sequencing of the components and objectives in a program. Obviously, if one act is believed to cause another act or effect, then it has to precede that other act or effect in time. However, Patton (1986) cautions that temporal sequencing not be exaggerated.

> Once a program is in operation, the relationships between links in the causal hierarchy are likely to be recursive rather than unidirectional. The implementation and attainment of higher-level objectives interact with the implementation and attainment of lower-order objectives through feedback mechanisms, interactive configurations, and cybernetic systems. Program components may be conceptually distinct in the formal version of a theory of action, but in practice these analytically distinct components, links, and stages are highly interdependent and dynamically interrelated. In short, the cause-effect relationships may be mutual, multidirectional, and multilateral. (p. 164)

For example, teaching methods used by CES educators to present information to clients affect their reactions which in turn affect the methods the teachers will use the next time; similarly, the climate in a public school classroom, e.g., the degree of discipline will affect the opinions of parents and the actions of parents and students, which will affect teachers and students and can change the climate in the classroom; and so on. As will be reiterated later on, the challenge is to describe program action as accurately as possible in a form that is useful.

THEORY AND MODELS

The theory suggested here is not the global, conceptual schemes of the grand theorists nor does it rest exclusively on proven social science theoretical schema (Chen and Rossi,

1983). What is advocated is defined by Shadish (1987) as microtheory--a description of the structural and operational characteristics of a program. As such, a program's theory does not have to be exactly like any other's; however, it is preferable that it be derived from empirical (and scientific) knowledge of the content domain for the program being described (Scheirer, 1987). In other words, "program theory" suggests there is a rationale or basis for believing certain outcomes will occur as a result of implementing certain activities.

Clarifying these basic assumptions is closer to what econometricians would call "model specification" than to what most social scientists would call general "theory development" (Chen and Rossi, 1983). And, in fact, the construction of models is what is advocated by most recent writers on the theory-driven approach to evaluation (e.g., Bickman, 1987b). The definitions for "program theory" are very similar to previous writers' definitions for "models," e.g.,

A good program theory will describe the elements and components of a program. ...(and) specify the relative importance of those elements (Bickman, 1987a, p. 11).

A model is a simplified representation of part of the "real world" that contains its most important relationships so that its essential workings may be studied (Rossini et al., 1981, p. 371).

The notion of models as used here does not <u>necessarily</u> carry with it the social science idea of generalizability, of explaining beyond the arena in/for which it was developed. The model should, however, represent the staff's perception of reality of whatever is being explained, i.e., it should be generalizable to whatever extent (level and/or pervasiveness) the program is defined or else there is not "a" program. The important implication for the EA process is not to worry about generalizability at the time the theory/model is being developed. If appropriate representatives of the different dimensions of the program are working on the theory, it is probably less stressful to just focus on their assumptions, on their attempts to solve some problem or achieve some goal.

de Geus (1988) was very emphatic in suggesting that generalizability not be a worry in these modeling experiences:

> God seems to have told model builders that a model should have predictive qualities and that therefore it should represent the real world. In building microworlds, however, this is totally irrelevant. What we want to capture are the models that exist in the minds of the audience. Almost certainly, these will not represent the real world. None of us has a model that actually captures the real world, because no complex reality can be represented analytically and a model is an analytical way of representing reality. Moreover, for the purpose of learning, it is not the reality that matters but the team's model of reality, which will change as members' understanding of their world improves (p. 73).

Models may have positive and negative features. Nonessential elements are excluded which allows the research focus to be narrowed--which is desirable, but sometimes, relevant aspects which do not fit within a given framework may be excluded--which can be undesirable (Rossini et al., 1981). The important task is to include any element necessary to explain how or why a program works. Whether or not it fits nicely into a graphic display of the theory is secondary to the requirement for explaining.

The model of program theory should contain those elements and components--under human control--considered necessary or sufficient for bringing about the desired impacts (Cook et al., 1985). Note the emphasis on manipulable variables. It does no good to include elements which cannot be changed or varied in some way. For example, knowing that a positive relationship exists between reading scores of youth and family income level does not enable a school system to improve its reading program because the school cannot affect a family's income. Similarly, knowing that water conservation programs produce greater water savings among residential consumers in communities characterized by higher educational levels is essentially irrelevant because a community's schooling is not subject to manipulation by the public officials trying to reduce water consumption (Berk, 1981).

MODEL FORMAT

A program theory model contains the essential components of the program connected in a causal sequence to ultimate outcomes. The actual format used to visually construct program theory is not as important as its information content. Initially, the EA team should use whatever format they feel comfortable with and which helps them to understand what the program is about. Later on, two other criteria become important: (1) communication clarity and ease with stakeholders, and (2) ease of analysis among the different program parts.

Whatever is used should be as simple as possible without losing important program information. The description should include all important steps identified to bring about the desired change and show the causal linkages, regardless of any preliminary assessment of program plausibility. Included are the identification of key components (sometimes expressed as intermediate objectives) that precede main goals, the activities and resources needed to bring about each component, and indicators of successful performance. Activities include client learning experiences, as well as legitimizing and promotional efforts, management strategies, and barrier reducers. The intent is to arrange these objectives, activities, and performance indicators into a causal, hierarchical, or time flow.

A basic model contains two parts: (1) a sequence of program logic with a supporting flow of (2) activities/functions, resources, and indicators of successful performance. A brief explanation of each part follows.

Program Logic

Expectations should be presented in such a way as to communicate the logic and flow of the program. There are a number of approaches for displaying a program's logic, e.g.,

Suchman's 1967 <u>Evaluation Research</u>, Patton's 1986 <u>Utilization Focused Evaluation</u>, Wholey's 1979 <u>Evaluation: Promise & Performance</u>. Suchman (1967) recommended constructing an objectives chain where immediate, intermediate, and ultimate goals are linked by priority of occurrence. Each level of objective represents the successful accomplishment of the one immediately preceding and is a precondition of the one following. Patton (1986) used this three-tier approach for an overview of the Minnesota Comprehensive Epilepsy Program and to focus information needs. A more detailed, multitiered chain of objectives was then developed for just those objectives where there was uncertainty or concern. Table 6-1 illustrates the initial three-tier conceptualization and the more refined multiplier chain.

Wholey (1979) suggested the format shown in Figure 6-1 for a logic model of a "typical government program." The boxes represent expected events and the arrows represent causal assumptions.

In the CES studies, key assumptions were listed in a time or causal sequence to form a hypothesis trail. Key components are enclosed in boxes connected with arrows which represent movement of program implementors and/or clients toward program goals. For example, the logic for CES' overall expectations may be diagrammed as a series of If-Then statements as in Figure 6-2. Another example is the logic model constructed for the Texas aquaculture program (Figure 6-3).

This kind of rational flow is sometimes not apparent until each of the supporting subsets of the program have been described and analyzed. However, for a program to exist there must be some kind of expectation that if program staff do certain things or provide services/benefits then other things will happen to clients and/or to program personnel and/or to the organization.

Activities, Resources, Performance Indicators

Each program component, in the If-Then chain is described in terms of purpose and what is required for

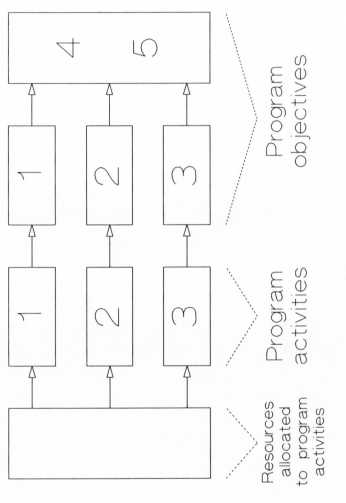

Figure 6-1.

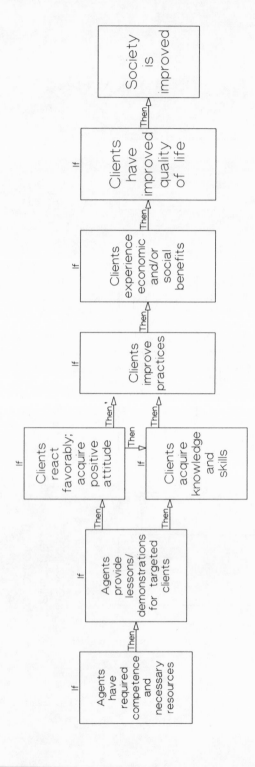

Figure 6-2. Overall logic model for extension programming.

Table 6-1.   Illustrative multi-tiered chain of objectives for the Minnesota Comprehensive Epilepsy Program (Patton, 1986, p. 155, minor adaptation of Table 7.1.

Initial Conceptualization:

Program Mission: To improve the lives of people with epilepsy through research.
Program Goal: To publish high quality, scholarly research on epilepsy.
Program Objective: To conduct research on neurological, pharmacological, epidemiological, and social psychological aspects of epilepsy.

Refined Conceptualization--from immediate (bottom) to ultimate (top) objectives:
1. Reduce epilepsy incidence and prevalence.
2. Provide better medical treatment for people with epilepsy.
3. Increase physicians' knowledge of better medical treatment for epileptics.
4. Disseminate findings to medical practitioners.
5. Publish findings in scholarly journals.
6. Produce high quality research findings on epilepsy.
7. Establish a program of high quality research on epilepsy.
8. Assemble necessary resources (personnel, finances, facilities) to establish a research program.
9. Identify and generate research designs to close knowledge gaps.
10. Identify major gaps in knowledge concerning causes and treatment of epilepsy.

accomplishment. This includes a listing of all the activities and resources that make a program happen--not just the learning opportunities for clients but all programming actions that are necessary for a change to occur, e.g., educational, legitimizing, and promotional activities; staff, hardware, information technology, supplies, and other necessary resources.

Performance indicators are descriptions of what can be observed that will capture implementation of activities and signal achievement of objectives and goals. Indicators are often not defined for program objectives and are even less likely to be defined for specific components and activities. Getting them defined can be frustrating for both the evaluator and the

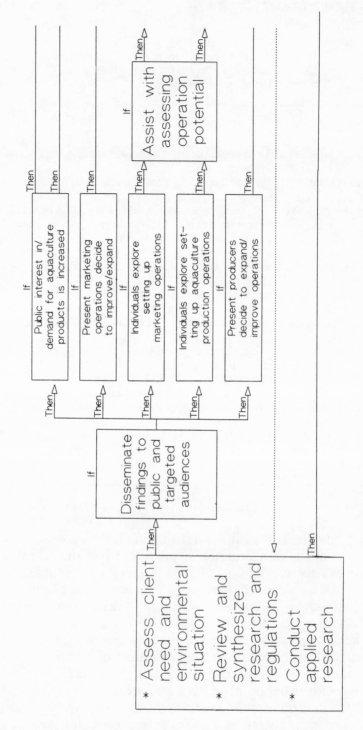

Figure 6-3. Logic model of Texas CES aquaculture program.

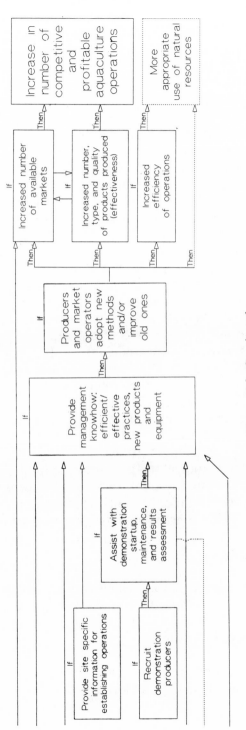

Figure 6-3. Continued.

program managers and implementors. There is sometimes a tendency for program staff, when caught with hazy objectives, to say to the evaluator: "You are the expert in evaluation; you tell us how to measure _____." This is a trap the evaluator should avoid as much as possible. Program personnel should define what will signal success of their program(s). "The analysis of objectives for 'measurability' is not, then, a test of the evaluator's ingenuity in defining measures. It is, rather, a test to determine whether the manager has defined what he wants his program to accomplish and what evidence he needs to determine this" (Schmidt et al., 1977, p. 75).

The last paragraph is not meant to suggest that evaluators sit by in stony silence while program staff struggle with performance indicators. It does mean, though, that the evaluator or EA leader should permit the staff to think through what they want to happen. Experience in the CES studies showed that a series of questions and gentle probes would start staff members thinking in the right direction. Also, insisting that they not worry about measurement at the beginning but rather just focus on any way they might know that something had occurred. This is an excellent time to brainstorm--to say anything that comes to mind--silly or not. A little levity will remove tension that usually builds up when "evidence" is discussed, and always seems to spark creativity.

Performance indicators are most helpful when they include optimum timing for measurements. For example some indicators and measurement points for three of the early components in CES' program logic (Figure 6-2) could be:

Prior to employment:

o   academic degrees of applicants are verified and/or
o   applicants are administered a knowledge test

After Agents hold lessons:

o   data are collected on number and type of program participants, learning materials, days expended, and resources expended o   program participants are administered a test on the content of programs.

This information could be diagrammed as shown in Figure 6-4 or it could be added to the narrative description along with the activities and resources. The latter procedure was followed in the EAs implemented in CES.

Figure 2-1 (pages 28-29) and Table 6-2 are examples of the two different parts of such a model using evaluability assessment as the "program." Figure 2-1 contains the tasks (components) arranged in a time/influence sequence and Table 6-2 shows the activities, resources, and indicators of performance for one of the key tasks.

CONSTRUCTING THEORY MODELS

How Many Models to Construct

Wholey (1979) described the development of four different models (and sometimes more than one of each) as tasks in the process of completing an EA: (1) the logic model to graphically represent the logical structure of the program; (2) the definitional model to identify the objectives management defined in measurable terms and evaluations that could be undertaken based on those measures; (3) the equivalency model to describe actual project operations in terms of feasible measures and to indicate the extent to which data are obtainable on these measures; and (4) the evaluable model which documents those portions of the program that can be feasibly measured and for which likely uses for performance information have been defined. Nay and Kay (1982) described the use of three models: logic, which displayed the basic assumptions; functional, which displayed the processes and events believed to occur to translate the logic to reality; and measurable, which displayed where measurements could be made to test assumptions and verify processes and events. Rog's (1985) synthesis of 57 EAs conducted in HHS and Education found three models to be common--a description of the program as stated and perceived, based on document

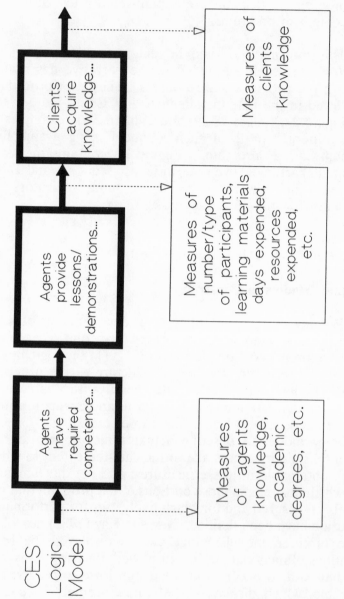

Figure 6-4.

Table 6-2. Supporting functional flow for one component in the logic model of evaluability assessment.

Task 5. Identify and interview stakeholders.

Activities	Measurement Indicators
1. Ask key administrators for names of potential stakeholders to interview	-- List of names of stakeholders by category
2. Convene staff and identify potential stakeholders and alternates by category; provide rationale for each choice	-- Record of training sessions including lesson plans
3. Name interviewer(s), train, if necessary	
4. Secure equipment for interviews: tape recorders, tapes, note pads	-- Appointment schedule of interviews
5. Set up procedures and schedule of activities with interviewer, e.g., how to record, to handle expenses, etc.	-- Copies of notes, tapes transcriptions
6. Conduct interviews	
7. Monitor interviewer(s), i.e., listen to tapes of interviews and/or scan notes; follow up with interviewer(s) to praise, suggest changes in or suggest changes in procedure and/or demeanor	
8. Transcribe notes or tapes	

Resources: --Travel for program personnel, at least 1/2 day per session, on average
--Tape recorder; one tape per 2 interviews, on average; transcription machine; note pads
--$50/interview, contractual basis, for travel, salary, phone calls, transcription, and other costs.

analysis and interviews of staff and decision makers; a depiction of the program as observed, based on visits to individual local project sites; and an evaluable model, based on all available information which displayed well-defined activities found to be implemented in a consistent manner and that had plausible goals and effects that could be reliably measured.

At the beginning of the CES studies, attempts were made to develop three models, similar to Nay and Kay (1982). The process just did not work. For example, knowledge was insufficient among program managers and other high level stakeholders to develop a definitional model, as described by Wholey (1979); program staff found it confusing to deal with several models; and sometimes too much effort seemed to be going to displaying information rather than to describing what went into them. This issue was resolved by developing ONE model of the program--one as close to implementation reality as possible.* As the previous sections described, the model contained two parts: an IF-THEN hypothesis trail of the logic and a functional section which contained activities and resources to translate that logic into reality and indicators of performance that were in place or could be with reasonable resources.

Who Should Define Program Theory

The implications of writings by one of the developers of EA is that evaluators define the theory of a program: "...These interactions are designed to ensure that the program theory developed by the evaluators..." (Wholey, 1987, p. 79). The intention of the Extension EAs was for program staff to do as much of the theory explication as possible. All the work did not ALWAYS get done in the presence of the team but that was the strived-for ideal.

Having program staff define the models was a result of three factors: (1) The decision was made early on to focus on one model of program theory--treatment as delivered. As just

---

*A second model was introduced by which to judge program plausibility. It is the staff's theory about the clients problem-solving process. This model is explained in Chapter Ten.

noted, developing several models was confusing to the team plus knowledge about the program was often too sparse among different stakeholder groups to develop other models for comparison. (2) Given that THE model to be developed was the actual one in operation, implementing staff were the most qualified for the task. The work team for each EA included up to five on-site program managers, with the majority--but not all-coming from very successful programs. The team members were usually in charge of the overall direction and day-to-day activities of the local programs. They decided what was and was not done in most instances and thus were very influential in shaping the philosophical bases of the treatments as implemented. (3) Program staff stand to benefit the most from the exercise (even though payoffs for the organization are also significant).

We did not understand the full ramifications of the last factor at the outset. Later it became clear that staff learned not only about the workings of their programs but also a new way of thinking about program development. de Geus (1988) suggested, and we found it to be true, that persons working together like this on models actually create a new language among themselves that expresses the knowledge they have all acquired. This creates an enormous amount of energy that translates directly to the organization in two ways. First, staff become more committed to the program and the organization--there is a camaraderie and a feeling of "belongingness" that develops among team members as they reveal assumptions and agree on common goals; plus, the actual model was a source of staff pride in each one of the CES EAs. Second, the program is improved.

Defining the Theory

Programs are complex undertakings with many elements and components that are not independent of each other. Programs that are implemented in several sites contain a variety of components, resources, and procedures which come together in as many ways as there are people who run them. Identifying the critical aspects of a program theory is a major task that is compounded by three factors: the value-laden aspect of programs, the uncertainty associated with complex problems, and the technical expertise of program staff. Because of these three factors, honest and thoughtful statements will emerge in these sessions only after understanding and trust has developed among team members.

Value-laden Aspects of Programs. Programs are"guided by traditions of common practice; ethical, religious, and political beliefs; and vague ideas about how to affect complex social processes" (Conrad and Miller, 1987, p. 23). Values determine goal implementation strategies and indicators selected to measure performance. This is one of the reasons it takes the core team a period of time to really get to work-- revealing assumptions of programs reveals basic beliefs of individuals about social problems, how participants become eligible recipients, and what "should" be done to try to help them. To paraphrase Gentry (1981): Any theory of a program is essentially a set of assumptions. Whether explicit or implicit, these assumptions dictate the programmer's approach with clients.

> Assumptions are the building blocks of a person's makeup and therefore of behavior. ...Assumptions guide the individual, determine what he or she will and will not do. They determine what the person expects or anticipates from self and others in any situation (Anderson, 1981, p. 779).

Uncertainty Associated with Complex Problems. The more complex a problem, the more assumptions that will have to be made--very few problems come directly to us preformulated from the gods:

> It is a characteristic, fundamental feature of real-world, as opposed to textbook problems that not everything of basic importance can be known prior to working on the problem. In the real world we do not start with a clear statement of the problem before we commence working on it. Rather a statement of the problem often emerges

only with difficulty over time and only as a direct result of our working on the problem (Mitroff, 1983).

Technical Expertise of Program Staff. The task of identifying program theory reveals a programmer's state of knowledge in the technical content area as well as in the program development process area.

Theory is developed in an EA through the use of conceptual categories and generalized relationships that emerge from program data (Wholey, 1987). Evaluators should begin by tentatively assuming a "muddy" program with uncertain delivery (Scheirer, 1987). The first order of business is to understand the working assumptions of those who actually carry out the program. These may or may not be the same as intended by program designers, nor what key stakeholders think they are or should be.

The exercise is best completed with a relatively small number of persons. (In CES, the group usually included one or two state-level content specialists, three to five local staff, the EA team leader, and often a high-level program administrator.) Those involved should have a close working knowledge of what the program is like in the field and represent differing levels of implementation of the program and/or differing clients or geographic areas. The intent here is to involve persons who can conceptualize the program pretty much in its entirety, while depending upon additional staff experience during validation to uncover omissions, inconsistencies, etc.

Data for the model may come from one-on-one interviews and/or from meetings where the several levels of program staff are together. The process for acquiring the data is secondary to what is acquired. However, developing models in open meetings can save a lot of time and work) and, as indicated earlier, be instructive to the program staff as well. Differences in program perspective may be reconciled on the spot and staff may learn a process for planning a program so it can be analyzed (and managed) for attainment of results.

Several sessions may be necessary to get the program framework described. Each session should be planned for <u>at least</u> a half day in length (preferably a full day or two) and should include the same individuals each time. Less than half-day sessions tend to end just as a group is really getting into the task--what with late arrivals and the normal time for redeveloping the mind set for productive work. Also, bringing in new people and updating absentees from previous sessions wastes a lot of time.

Exactly how the open sessions are conducted to arrive at a consensus model of the program will vary with the individuals involved--mostly by the style of the EA leader. The procedure followed in the Extension EAs required the use of flip charts and chalk boards. Items were listed on a chalk board until tentative decisions were reached as to where they fit in the model; they were then written on paper and taped on the wall. As the conceptualization of the theory unfolds, items move around. What was thought initially to be a key component may turn out to be a support activity and vice versa and some may not seem to fit anywhere. This is okay. The primary consideration the first time through is to get parts of the program identified.

The procedure for constructing the model can begin in the middle or on either end of the IF-THEN hypothesis chain. The more rational approach is from an end but, as indicated earlier, some programs are more rationally conceived than others. The intended outcome of the EA will also influence where one begins. If the intent is to plan a program, the logical flow may begin with the end point (goal) and "back up" as a sequence of cause and strategy for change are determined.

The Maryland water program--which was a planning effort--will be used here to demonstrate this process. That program resulted in four different problem-solving models, one for each target audience. Each went through several iterations. The process proceeded as follows:

1. For each targeted audience, the end goals were listed and the question asked: "What does this audience have to do to make these goals a reality?" To answer this question, the team had to decide what was in the power of that particular audience to do something about. For example, the team identified three types of management practices that could be

implemented by agricultural producers to help resolve the water problem:

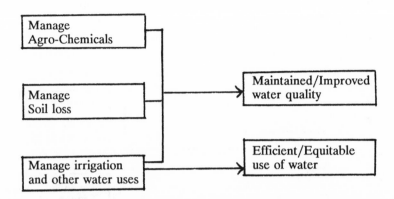

2. A similar question was asked about these key events as was asked about the end goals: "What has to happen for agricultural producers to implement these practices?" Again there were three answers:

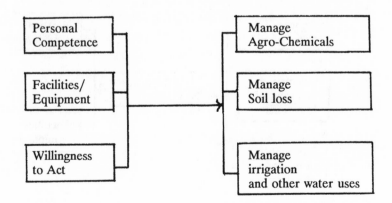

3. For each of these last three key events, the same question was asked: "What has to happen for agricultural producers to acquire the personal competence (knowledge and skills) and any special facilities and equipment, and then be willing to act?" It was decided that willingness to act had to precede the acquisition of competence and facilities and equipment:

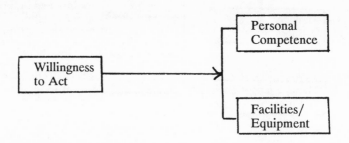

And, willingness to act would be motivated by expectation of profit, fear of being jailed or fined, and/or concern for social good:

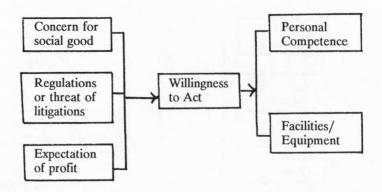

This type of process continued:

o   Concern for social good would require awareness of the present problem and some understanding of the future scenario if improvement measures are not taken.

o   For regulations to become a motivating factor, the producers would have to know what the laws are, what the personal impact on them and their business would be if they did not comply, and what future restrictions might be imposed.

o   For an expectation of profit, dollar incentives may have to be created and whatever ones are available would have to be known to the producers--known in the sense that the producers know they are available, they know how to access them, and they believe it is economically advantageous to their operations to access them.

o   All three of these requirements are impacted by legislative action and by policy development by public agencies.

o   The legislature and public agencies are moved to act by citizen pressure and by concern for social good. And, public officials and citizens require some understanding of the present and expected scenario of the water problem--in Maryland specifically and where the Chesapeake Bay is concerned, to its furtherest outreaches.

The logical analysis demonstrated above was repeated for each audience. The model which resulted for agricultural producers is produced as Figure 6-5.

How a problem is conceived in terms of cause will determine audience expectations, key components and expectations of the program, and the content and timing of educational activities. And, as Bickman (1987a) pointed out, there may be more than one correct theory just as there may be more than one cause for a problem. The important task is to get A theory developed so IT can be tested.

If the EA goal is to model reality as implemented, the procedure might be different. For example, the Illinois, California, and Maryland 4-H studies proceeded as follows:

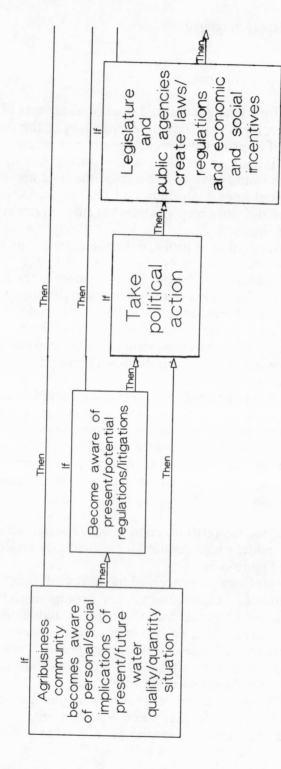

Figure 6-5. Program model for agricultural producers in Maryland's water quality/quantity program.

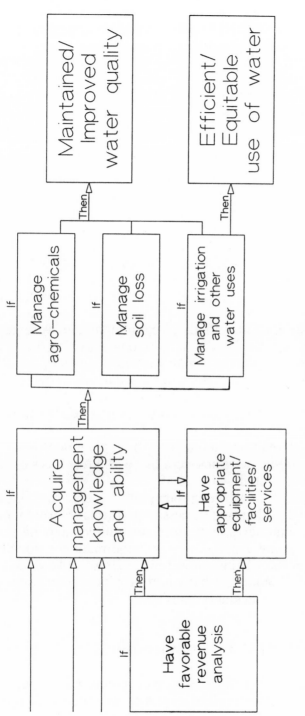

Figure 6-5. Continued.

First, staff who implemented the program were asked to tell "everything you do. Take any week--what did you do each day?" Listing continued until they could think of nothing they do that was not written down.

Second, the activities were grouped according to larger elements by asking "What does this activity lead to? What happens before it? What comes after?"

Third, effects were identified. For example, in the Maryland 4-H program, the staff listed effects on youth members, on families of members, on volunteers, on communities, and on society.

Fourth, elements and effects were arranged into a sequential framework. This is the logic portion of the model. Only those parts which the staff believed to be directly connected to their goals or intended effects were included. Any that did not seem to fit were saved--in case a later connection was identified. Team members were asked to identify rationale for the superfluous activities, i.e., to think about why they did them and what consequences the activities might have. (This exercise can help staff see activities that are irrelevant to what they are trying to accomplish. They may continue to do them, but at least they will be able to prioritize with some knowledge of potential effect.)

Fifth, each component in the logic model was checked to make sure all activities were listed and resources used to get them implemented were specified.

Sixth, for each component and effect in the logic model, sources and evidence of successful performance were identified. For the components, indicators and sources may be listed for each supporting activity or just for the main component. The overall question being answered is "How could we know this happened?" Who or what could provide the evidence and of what would the evidence consist?

Validate Model with Staff Experience

After a program has been developed with input from the different program levels, it should be validated with experience from local implementation sites. In CES that usually meant contacting county faculty and in some cases, trained volunteers--whoever it was that delivered the program to clients.

Validation is an iterative process. It can take place by visits to selected sites for individual input or in open forums where several sites/persons at a time may participate. The latter procedure can provide input in a shorter time, plus when several people are present, individuals seem more willing to point out weaknesses and inconsistencies in the initial conceptualization of the program. Needed changes are made to the description after each iterative session to prevent the waste of time of several people identifying the same weaknesses/omissions.

Whether individually or in a group, persons reviewing the program model should first specify the objectives for the program as implemented in their locale(s). If their objectives are essentially the same as already identified, they can review the "finished" model and suggest where they think the description is at variance with (their) reality.

Careful analyses should be made during this step to determine if one model is appropriate or if more than one is needed. Very large differences should not occur among staff carrying out the same program even though they are at different sites. Each one will verbalize essentially the same goals and objectives and have planned about the same overall events and activities but no two will be exactly alike. While this makes management and evaluation difficult to perform and accountability elusive, it is a condition that should be expected in agencies where programs are locally based and controlled. The point to remember here is that this model is not an exact replica of every single nitty gritty aspect of a program. However, it should accurately reflect the major assumptions undergirding the program, and the critical activities that are going on in the different places in which it is being implemented.

Just how close an actual program has to be in comparison to its initial proposal or plan before it can be said to be implemented is not an easy question to answer. When there is great divergence or when essentially nothing is going on, the question is easy. Otherwise, it is not. Programs take shape over a period of time, sometimes with different leaders, in an environment of multiple uncertainties and emerging complexities--and each environment pushes and pulls on a program with differing results. The evaluator or EA leader should not make this decision alone, decision makers should be involved in clarifying the amount of difference to be tolerated between ideal and real implementation. (Patton, 1986; Williams and Elmore, 1976).

> For a complex treatment package put in different local settings, decisionmakers usually will not expect--or more importantly, <u>not want</u>--a precise reproduction of every detail of the package. The objective is performance, not conformance. However, in the ideal situation, those responsible for implementation would take the basic idea and modify it to meet special local conditions. There should be a reasonable resemblance to the basic idea, as measured by inputs and expected outputs incorporating the best of the decision and the best of the local ideas. (Williams and Elmore, 1976, p. 277-278)

There are no criteria for how much similarity is enough. However, where substantial variations are found to exist, when implementation integrity becomes an issue, it is not for the evaluator or EA team to decide alone. It is a question for policy makers and program managers to debate. They must decide if it is acceptable for more than one program to exist within a larger framework. More than one evaluation design can be employed to measure these disparate programs, but the question is whether anyone wants such variation to continue. They must decide how much difference between real and ideal will be tolerated.

Deciding how many persons (sites) to involve in the validation may take some careful thinking when an impact study is anticipated for a program implemented in many sites. When only a few sites are involved, it is easier. The number required depends partially on how much variation is expected from one locale to the next and how many levels of a program are being checked.

Since there is always a trade-off between what can be learned and resources that can be expended, one procedure would be to initially select representatives from six to ten program sites in addition to those represented by the EA program team. Begin with sites which represent extremes in the program. Start with two or three sites. If differences are few and/or minor, no other sites may be contacted. If differences are significant, contact two or three other sites. Continue until there is a degree of satisfaction that the program described is or is not the one operating in the field. As noted above, key decision makers may need to assist with the latter conclusion.

Writers on EAs conducted in other areas (e.g., Nay and Kay, 1982; Wholey, 1979) definitely recommend that sample activities/events be observed in the field. However, direct observation may be unnecessary or at least minimal for some programs, if the validation steps in this chapter are carefully implemented. Two reasons support this recommendation.

One: If the "walk-in" validation process with staff experience reveals a lack of major agreement on overall logic and key activities, a (single) program probably does not exist. Observations in the field, in this instance, would be a waste of resources just as surely as would proceeding with an evaluation. (Unless, of course, the purpose of the evaluation is to secure evidence to eliminate a program!)

Two: When the model is being developed and when it is being validated, the EA leader can usually determine if input persons are clear with their descriptions. This is especially the case when the performance indicators are being identified. A question like "If a key stakeholder visited your program and said 'Show me your evidence for this event,' what could you deliver?" moves the discussion from "what could be an indicator" to "what specific evidence could you provide." Most local CES staff can readily provide such things as newspaper clippings and rosters of participants. Such are evidence of the event being implemented.

There are no specific guidelines for recognizing when direct observation is necessary but the implementation example in Table 6-3 shows the complexity of determining implementation validity and hopefully will prepare one for the intensity of the probing that is required. The differences between what was planned and what was implemented at any one of the sites would make some or all of the planned outcomes unattainable or unmeasurable. For example, at Site 1, the program staff may be lucky if 100 people show up--that is far short of their goal of 500. Also, those who do show may already have reason to believe they are at risk--so the program may not really meet a need of identifying new "at risk" clients. At Site 2, too little information may be generated by the reduced number of tests to provide sufficient evidence for the participants to be diagnosed "at risk" and/or for them to be motivated to see their physicians. At Site 3, the positive outcomes may occur but there will be no way to prove it.

Obviously, if the reviewer observed three health fairs and observed these three results, the inclusion of health fairs as a component to gather data on an evaluation would be suspect. If similar findings were found in one of three, it would be cause to check a little further.

Table 6-3. Implementation of Health Fair.

An event in a health program was a two-day Health Fair in a city mall. The intent was to have registered nurses and medical doctors administering tests and making diagnoses which would suggest to participants if they were at risk for hypertension, adult onset diabetes, etc. The expected outcome was to identify persons who did not suspect they were "at risk." Five hundred people were expected to be tested and diagnosed and 90% of those found "at risk" were expected to contact their personal physicians for confirmations of the diagnoses and for advice, if needed.

Observations of the planned event showed:

Site 1. The event was held at the community center but other parts were implemented as planned.

Analysis: Not the same audience as planned.

Site 2. Volunteer homemakers instead of nurses administered pressure checks and took histories. Other tests were cancelled.

Analysis: Too few tests to make planned "at risk" recommendations.

Site 3. Everything was as planned except too few volunteers showed up to get participant names and addresses.

Analysis: Planned outcome not measurable without ability to follow up on those judged "at risk."

CHAPTER SEVEN

Identify and Interview Stakeholders

For an evaluability assessment or an impact study to begin, someone must make an inquiry about a program. That inquiry may come from one or more sources, e.g., elected officials, administrators, program managers or staff, or citizen groups. Regardless of who does the initial asking, a variety of other people will be interested in and can be expected to have differing views about the program under study and about any potential future evaluation. These persons are called "stakeholders." Evaluations start and stop with one or more of these individuals. They generally request the evaluative information and when it is generated (to their satisfaction), they use it. Some stakeholders will be served directly; others will simply want to be consulted and kept informed.*

---

*Among the stakeholders, there is typically a primary client who has responsibility and accountability for the evaluation exercise. However, there are situations where there is no single client who sponsors the evaluation and whose needs must be met first and foremost. The CES cases in this book fall somewhere between these two. Because of the nature of the project (to adapt EA to a field-based programming organization), there was no one client who requested each of the EAs and felt accountable for them. There was, though, stakeholders identified whose needs held priority over those of others.

DEFINITION OF A STAKEHOLDER

Stakeholders are those persons or groups who impact a program in very significant ways or who are similarly affected by the actions of a program. They are "...those interest groups, parties, actors, claimants, and institutions--both internal and external to the corporation--that exert a hold on it" (Mitroff, 1983, p. 4).

A stakeholder is not just anyone with information needs and therefore a potential evaluation user. Rather, they are persons with vested interest in a program whose decisions can affect the program's future in very important ways. Specifically, stakeholders include funding organizations, legislative bodies, boards of directors, public interest groups, and program administrators/staff. Cook et al. (1985) describe stakeholders as groups:

> ...keen to preserve or promote their interests...to see certain issues on action agendas and not others; ...to see problems defined their own way and not in some different way; ...routinely prefer that some solutions be tried over others...that some criteria are measured over others, that some standards of comparison are chosen over others, and that some techniques of measuring performance and integrating information are selected rather than others. ...want the right to be heard in the formal and informal deliberations from which decisions about program changes emerge. ...want to be able to represent their interests--and perhaps influence decisions--irrespective of what the evaluative data seem to say (p. 702).

In short, stakeholders are people whose interests or stakes in programs can be lost, improved, protected, or treated fairly or unfairly (Greene, 1987b) and whose actions relative to the program will be influenced by how their interests/stakes are treated.

RATIONALE FOR STAKEHOLDER INPUT

Four tasks are described in this chapter: identify stakeholders, prepare interview questions, select interviewer(s), and conduct interviews. Before these tasks are discussed, though, the rationale for seeking stakeholder input needs to be clarified, for that understanding impacts the planning and implementation of each of the tasks, and the outcome of the entire evaluability assessment.

The primary reason for seeking stakeholder input relates to the first goal of every organization--to survive (Gross, 1968). In the programming context, this means surviving in as good a fashion as possible such that the other important goals of the program (organization) can be achieved. Stakeholders can make decisions that affect a program's continuation (survival) but the more common type of decision is one which affects the fashion in which it survives, i.e., changes in direction and changes in resource allocation. For either type of decision, it is critical that key actors be identified whose standards and beliefs about the program are the most influential and to identify the criteria by which that influence is proffered.

The overall reason, then, for involving stakeholders is to acquire the ability, at some later time, to "influence the influencers." If it is known who makes decisions that affect programs, what those decisions are, and the bases on which those decisions are made, then efforts to influence will be more successful and use fewer resources.

When stakeholders are contacted, it should be <u>very clear</u> to the interviewer and to the stakeholder that the purpose of the interview is <u>to secure information from them</u>--NOT to provide them with information. This means, first, that they are asked their perceptions and they can give no wrong answers. It is not the time to try to change any perceptions they describe that may be at odds with what the interviewer believes to be the "truth" as concrete, objective data would show a situation to be. The intent is to find out from them what they believe. Action to change those beliefs, if warranted, should come at another time. Stakeholders are not as apt to be open with their thoughts if it becomes apparent that there are "right" answers and when that occurs, all the resources invested in the interviews will have been wasted and perhaps even worse, the organization may act on assumptions that are at odds with reality.

Second, it means that persons selected for interviews should be aware of the program, have some knowledge about it, and have the potential for using data collected about program performance. They should not be sent information about the program prior to the interview. If they are true stakeholders, they have been making decisions that impacted the program (organization) and sending them prior information, if anything, will only prepare them to give "acceptable" answers and prevent our knowing on what bases they actually decide.

Third, it means they are asked questions they are qualified to answer: perceptions about an existing program, assessments of the need for and appropriateness of objectives for an existing or a planned program, concerns about how an existing program is being implemented and/or about how it is accomplishing (or not) its goals, adequacy of resources for an existing program, and needs for evaluative information for an existing or a planned program.

Only in very rare instances would non program staff be asked to suggest specific approaches to accomplish goals or how to evaluate a program. In addition to many of them not having the experience on which to base answers to these questions, asking them can decrease stakeholder confidence in the organization's ability to deliver the program, i.e., cause them to doubt if program staff know what they are doing. There are some stakeholders who, though not program staff, will be well informed about such things and with whom "how-to" questions can be pursued. However, experience on the CES studies suggests that their time may better be spent on the content identified in the previous paragraph.

Fourth, it means that the interviewer(s) are selected for their interviewing capability--NOT for their knowledge of the program under review. They should be attentive listeners and competent probers. They should not have any obvious stake in the program, themselves. If they do, even if they are truly objective, stakeholders may be reluctant to say what they think, especially if they have any negative thoughts.

With these admonitions clearly in mind, the tasks of identifying and interviewing stakeholders can proceed.

IDENTIFY STAKEHOLDERS

Identifying the persons who have a stake in a program and its evaluation is not as simple as it might seem. Nay and Kay (1982) indicate that part of the difficulty is a result of the paucity of decision makers in government programs. They assert that there are many more position takers than decision makers. At any rate, the place to start is with whoever requested the information. After that, several approaches can be used (e.g., see Dunn et al., 1981; Lawrence and Cook, 1982; Mitroff, 1983; Nay and Kay, 1982; Patton, 1984).

Nay and Kay (1982) recommend following the flow of money and/or information through a system. For example, in Extension, funds originate at three levels: in Congress and through the USDA-ES structure to state land-grant colleges where additions are made from state appropriations on to county offices where additions are made from county governments. Information flows show the movement of pertinent data as they move from one location to another.

Mitroff (1983) suggested the following identification procedures:

o   Imperative: persons who feel strongly enough about an organization to act on their feelings. These could be supportive or defiant. Sources of these imperatives, slogans, catch words, and acts are potential stakeholders.

o   Positional: persons that occupy formal positions in the organizational policy-making structure. Organizational charts and legal documents are good sources for this method.

o   Reputational: a sociometric process which entails asking various knowledgeable or important persons to nominate others whom they believe to have a stake in the program or the evaluation.

o Socio-participation: individuals who participate in program policy activities, e.g., advisory committees, special interest groups.

o Opinion-leadership: those who tend to shape the opinions of other stakeholders, e.g., editors of newspapers, magazines, and journals.

o Demographic: identifies stakeholders by characteristics such as age, race, sex, occupation, religion, educational level, income level, etc.

o Focal organizational: those with important relationships with the organization or program, e.g., suppliers, employees, clients, allies, competitors, and regulators and controllers.

The procedure(s) selected will depend upon a number of factors including resources for the EA (money, people, time), openness of the program staff to differing points of view, and the political prominence of the program (Lawrence and Cook, 1982). Each approach will include some persons that others miss. It is suggested that more than one approach be used since "different stakeholders do not generally share the same definition of an organization's 'problems' and hence, they do not in general share the same 'solutions'" (Mitroff, 1983, p. 5). They have their own models of both what they do and what others do.

Once the stakeholders are identified, the list should be prioritized. The first and foremost priority is obviously to the individual(s) who sponsored the evaluability assessment. Criteria for inclusion of others--or in instances where there is no obvious primary client--include (1) perception of the potential harm or benefit each stakeholder can exert on the program, the organization, and the evaluation; and (2) the knowledge/interest each one has about/in the program and/or the evaluation. Persons may be excluded from the list because they are judged to be low on either or both of the criteria or because their views are adequately represented by other stakeholders.

Mitroff (1983, pp. 35-39) listed seven key propositions which described his assumptions about intrinsic and extrinsic properties of stakeholders. One of these propositions included a number of categories for describing a stakeholder's behavior. Though these categories were not offered by Mitroff as a prioritization tool, the majority of the categories could be used for making comparisons among stakeholders for that purpose, e.g.,

1. their purposes and motivations, as they pertain to the program;
2. their special knowledge and opinions;
3. their commitments, legal and otherwise;
4. their relationships to other stakeholders by virtue of power, authority, responsibility, and accountability; and
5. the resources at their command, e.g.,
   --material,
   --symbolic (pertaining to political office),
   --physical,
   --positional (e.g., place in a social or informational network),
   --informational (e.g., access to special or privileged sources); and
   --skills.

A discussion by Pearsol (1987) suggested other criteria that might be helpful for prioritization. Select those:

o who have a stake in a major versus minor program component,
o who affect more versus fewer people,
o in a position for concrete action-oriented use of information about the program,
o for which follow-through on actual use is more likely,
o with uncertainty reduction capabilities.

The number to involve will be a consideration of the priority setting mentioned above and a consideration of the resources of the EA team. The more people who are involved, the more work for the team. Nay and Kay (1982) suggest including those from the lowest level of the program up through one level above the purchaser of the evaluative information. For example, if a county director wanted evaluative information on a program, expectations would be checked for program participants, volunteer staff, agents, the county director, and the district or regional supervisor. If the regional director wanted the information, then all the levels just listed plus at least one above the regional director would be contacted. The rationale for this rule is that purchasers generally want information not only for their own use but to impress someone further up in the organization. Therefore, at least some of the evidence the purchaser considers appropriate is that which his/her supervisor values. Secondly, if the information is to be used, it must be implemented with or by those below the purchaser. Thus, it must be the kinds of evidence that they will find convincing.

Combining these approaches for the CES Texas aquaculture producer program resulted in an initial listing of 106 stakeholders. This list was reduced to 32 by prioritizing on two criteria: how much the team thought an individual stakeholder knew and cared about the CES aquaculture program and how much influence they were perceived to have on the program.

PREPARE INTERVIEW QUESTIONS

The questions to ask stakeholders are rather specific. They must provide information to achieve one of the two primary outcomes from an EA:

Identification of stakeholder awareness of and interest in a program, i.e., their perceptions of what a program is meant to accomplish, their concerns/worries about a program's progress toward total attainment, their perceptions of adequacy of program resources, and their interests in or needs for evaluative information on a program.

As indicated at the beginning of this chapter, the questions should secure information from the stakeholders. And, open-ended questions are better for that purpose than those that provide simple answer alternatives, e.g., Yes-No questions are almost never appropriate <u>unless</u> additional probing is planned.

Another rule offered at the beginning of this chapter was that questions should be about what stakeholders are qualified to answer. Note differences in the questions in Table 7-1 which were asked of business leaders, state officials, and University administrators, stakeholders of the Maryland 4-H program, and those in Table 7-2 which were asked of local program staff in the Illinois county officials program. The program staff questions ask for specifics about how they work and how the program is functioning; the questions for the "higher-level" Maryland program stakeholders do not.

The specific questions may be worded differently as long as they secure the information needed for the outcome defined above. Also, other questions may be added based on gaps revealed in the review of written materials and/or from data needs generated as the interviews progress. To reduce error in interviewee response, the following suggestions are offered:

o   Think of the respondent when wording the questions. The language and complexity should reflect the capability of the respondent to understand and provide meaningful responses. The questions should be checked to ensure that there is only one interpretation; a pretest should be undertaken with respondents from the same population which is to be studied or one that is similar in relevant aspects. Obtain respondent insight about the questions; make alterations and pretest again (if necessary). (Dillman, 1978; Summerhill, 1983)

o   Make the questions as simple, direct, and precise as the situation requires (Bradburn, 1982; Cantwell, 1983). Some questions like "What are your overall perceptions of the program?" are meant to be broad to elicit a wide array of responses. Other questions like "What do you think the missions goals are?" are meant to be very specific.

SELECT INTERVIEWER(S)

Persons selected to conduct interviews should be selected for their interviewing capability. They should not have any obvious stake in the program, or at least, they should have as little as possible. For example, in CES, this means that advisory committee members, state specialists, and county staff working in the program studied should not conduct the interviews. The idea is to have stakeholders speak freely about the program and they may not be willing to do that if they perceive the interviewer to be committed to the program. They may be reluctant to be completely open for fear of hurting the interviewer's feelings or for fear of giving "wrong" answers.

The interviewer(s) should be carefully selected. Those with little patience, who do not speak clearly or are not interested in the subject matter or the process make poor interviewers and should not be selected.

Table 7-1. Interview Questions for Maryland 4-H Evaluability Assessment

---

For Business Leaders, State Officials, and University Administrators

1. What are your overall perceptions of the 4-H program in Maryland?
2. What do you think the mission (goals) are and/or should be?
3. Who is the 4-H audience? Who is served (or should be) by the program?
4. What are the effects of the program on its audience? How are they different as a result of being in the program?
5. What do you think about how the program is implemented, strategies that are used, or activities? Do you have any concerns about these?
6. What are your perceptions about the resources of the program? Are they adequate? (If person says "No," ask: What more is needed?)
7. Do you have any need for data about the program? If the program were to undergo further evaluation, do you have questions that you would like answered? (If "Yes," ask: What would you like to know? How do you prefer to acquire that information? When do you need to have the information?
8. Is there anything else I should know? Are there others I should talk with about 4-H?

Table 7-2. Interview Questions for Illinois Public Officials EA.

For local program staff

Goals and Objectives
1. What do you think the TeleNet* programs are trying to accomplish?
2. What changes or differences, if any, is this program making with regard to participants, county advisers, the community, and/or the county.
3. What negative effects, if any, might the program have or be having? (If some are mentioned, ask: What do you think could/should be done to avoid these negative effects?)
4. When did the program start? When do you expect it to end?

Tasks and Activities
5. What tasks do you perform with the program (or what is the program expected to do to bring about expected changes)?
6. How do each of these tasks contribute to accomplishing the objectives?
7. What problems, if any, do you face in performing these tasks? (If problems are identified, ask: What do you think could or should be done to overcome these problems?)
8. What other organizations or persons are involved with you in this program (or with whom do you work in performing these tasks)?
9. Does anything need to be changed to improve working relationships?
10. How do you let board members know about the program?
11. To what extent do you feel you reach the target audience?

Resources
12. What resources are used or are available at the local level to carry out the different program activities?
13. How adequate are these resources? What, if any, additional or different help or resources are needed?

Performance Indicators/Further Evaluation
14. What are your feelings about this program being evaluated?
15. What are some of the indicators of success that the evaluation might try and measure? When could they be measured?
16. Are there any questions or concerns about the program operation or results that you would like to see addressed by an evaluation?
17. What would you like to see happen as a result of an evaluation? What use, if any, would you make of evaluation findings on this program?
18. Who would you like to impress or influence with evaluation findings?
19. What types of information or evidence is likely to impress these persons?

General
20. Is there anything else I should know or anything you would like to add?

---

*TeleNet was the shortened name for the Illinois program for local elected public officials. Different sites were connected via telephone.

Once selected, the interviewers(s) should be trained in general interviewing techniques. Some of the pitfalls to plan to avoid are included in the next section on conducting interviews.

How many interviewers are employed in an EA is dependent upon several factors, e.g., resources available to the EA, number of people to be interviewed, types (levels of importance) of people to be interviewed, and competencies of available interviewers. There are advantages to having one person do them all--if that person is skillful--because then the same prejudices and biases should occur in all interviews. There are also disadvantages, e.g., only one person's perspectives of stakeholders is captured and more time will be required for conducting and analyzing the interviews.

In some instances, more than one interviewer may be almost mandatory. For example, in the Maryland 4-H EA, some of the stakeholders held positions which made it important that a person with some recognized status in the organization (but not identified with the program) conduct their interviews, e.g., the Governor's aide to education, the State Comptroller, the Secretary of the Department of Agriculture, and so on. This same person could not give the time to conduct all the interviews, so an interviewer had to be hired for the less-sensitive interviews.

CONDUCT INTERVIEWS

Interviews begin after the study of written material on the program has started. An interview schedule should be developed to ensure that each interviewee makes input on all important points. "In this part of the evaluation process, the (interviewer) must obtain enough time from (the stakeholders) to ensure that he or she understands their objectives and expectations for the program and the important issues that surround the program" (Wholey, 1979, p. 53).

Some writers (e.g., Nay and Kay, 1982) suggest that mail surveys can be used to secure information on intended program logic. That is not recommended here. The response rate to such questionnaires may be too low and/or lack full response to individual questions and yield incomplete data. Busy people are more likely to take time to verbally answer questions than they are to write out the detail that is needed for an EA. Also, any mailed list of questions can only include what the asker knows to ask. The person being queried may have intimate knowledge of areas not previously uncovered. In an interview, these can be probed and result in a much richer description of program concerns, processes, or impacts.

Mail questionnaires may be useful in combination with personal interviews, as a way to validate what was learned in the interviews and to get some level of input from a larger number of people than time and other resources would allow for personal interviews. This combined use of both approaches for securing data can also extend the range of ownership for and interest in a study. However, mail questionnaires should not be used instead of personal interviews. If funds for collecting data are scarce, either the list of stakeholders should be decreased or the EA should not be pursued.

INSURE THAT DATA ARE VALID AND USEFUL

The bottom line in any evaluation is the validity of the data on which conclusions are based, and evaluability assessments are no exception. One method for securing data for EAs is through interviews. If data from these interviews are to be valid, the interviewers must know what they are doing and they must constantly be alert as to the goals of the study. The advice necessary to conduct valid and reliable interviews can only be touched on in this text. Two texts with more detailed information on this subject are Patton's (1980) Qualitative Evaluation Methods and Guba and Lincoln's (1981) Effective Evaluation.

All the main elements of an interview provide instances for affecting the credibility of data: the questions asked and their wording, the interview situation, the interviewee, and the interviewer (Weiss, 1975). Conditions to avoid on the questions have already been considered. Here the next three elements will be discussed.

The Interview Situation

The time and place of the interview can affect stakeholder responses as can procedures used to record the interviews. Steps to increase data credibility are:

o   Secure commitment of adequate time for an unhurried interview. Work around the stakeholder's schedule as much as possible.
o   Conduct interviews one-on-one and in private. It is desirable to have interviewees' full attention and for them to be able to speak freely. Third parties may distract the interviewee and/or constrain the range of responses.
o   Be prepared for the interview. Have interview schedule, a notebook, pen, etc., at hand.
o   Ensure that the respondent is comfortable with the procedure adopted. For example, some persons may be inhibited by tape recorders. Lots of times, though, once the interview is underway, they will forget and begin to speak freely. Assuring these persons about the purpose of the interview, how their responses will be treated, and respecting their privacy will go far in building trust--which use of a taping device requires.

The Interviewee

Individuals are purposely selected for interview in an EA because they are knowledgeable about the workings of the program and/or because they are presumed to have influence on the program. Thus the usual concerns about sample size (number of the population interviewed) and selection bias are not applicable here. Unless, of course, the persons nominating interviewee candidates know of negative effects from a program and intentionally avoid naming stakeholders who have that knowledge.

In some agencies where EAs are requested by non-program persons, the latter "whitewash" situation might be attempted. But, in EAs conducted to ascertain the full range of stakeholders' perceptions of a program--so any necessary corrective action can be taken--such obvious biasing action would be illogical.

Respondents may give wrong (untrue) answers to questions about a program if they do not understand the purpose of the interview. For example, if they believe data are being collected to reduce or eliminate a program they support, they may intentionally paint a more positive picture than actually exists. Some respondents will do this by simply omitting from the discussion anything that could be construed as negative, i.e., give only positive examples. Others may actually fabricate or skew responses. To decrease these incidents, the interviewer should:

o   Explain the purposes of the EA at the start of the interview. Indicate that the intent is to determine if weaknesses exist, so they can be eliminated, and to identify strengths, so they can be emphasized. That should be easy to do since that is the truth!

Respondents may try to guess what the interviewer wants to hear and say that--sometimes for the reasons stated above and sometimes because they simply want to please. In these--or to avoid such instances--the interviewer should:

o   Avoid phrases that may be construed as appreciative, e.g., "that's good," in favor of value-neutral remarks such as "What you are saying is" and then repeat the essence of the response.

The Interviewer

The interviewer may be a source of a number of potential errors. S/He may have preconceived notions about a program, which can lead to asking leading questions, to anticipation of stakeholder response, and selective recording of response statements. To prevent these problems the interviewer should:

o   Identify personal biases before starting interviews. One
    way to do this is to write out anticipated responses to
    the interview questions.   Then, in the interview,
    intentionally listen for responses that may be different.
o   Let the person being interviewed do the talking. Do not
    second guess them or lead them or automatically help
    them if they are reaching for a concept or phrase. Let
    them think and speak for themselves.

Interviewers may also have inadequate communication
skills, e.g., poor listening (not hearing what is really said) and
talking too much. Poor listening can lead to ambiguous and/or
incomplete answers. Talking too much can turn off and/or tire
the respondent, can lead the interview into irrelevant areas,
and can tax the available time, leading to hurried responses.
The interviewer should:

o   Think about what the respondent is saying and make
    sure that questions are answered, as well as that the
    respondent has actually finished what he/she wanted to
    say.
o   Avoid intruding into the interview.   Remember, the
    respondent is the expert about his/her perceptions. Do
    not give explanations or examples except those that were
    approved in training or in discussions with the EA task
    force.

The interviewer should listen carefully to everything the
stakeholders say. Persons from each level in the organization
will see a program from the perspective of that level's functions
and needs.

When those in charge discuss their programs, careful
notice should be taken of the range, or scope, of the
issues they discuss, the actions they consider to be
available, the problems they see as important, and the
performance information they already know or are
interested in. The range of the program as carried in
their minds, the possibilities of action as perceived by
them, and the range of activities in which they see

themselves as being involved help to delimit their particular island as they see it. Combined with other intelligence, such information contains essential clues both to the further interaction necessary to enable later use of the evaluation results and to parameters of design. (Nay and Kay, 1982, pp. 103-104)

One last bit of advice for the interviewer:

o   Allow time to expand and annotate your notes IMMEDIATELY following the interview. They may be incomprehensible several hours later. Even if a tape recorder is used, the relevance of comments may be lost after several days/weeks have elapsed. This also allows for any needed follow-up to the interview--while it is still fresh on the mind of the interviewee.

CHAPTER EIGHT

Describe Stakeholder Perceptions of Program

The perceptions of stakeholders need to be described for comparison with each other and with the detailed program implementation model. Many stakeholders may know little about the specific activities of a program but will have some idea about overall goals and some of the key components. Some will have more intimate knowledge than others.

ANALYZE AND SUMMARIZE STAKEHOLDER INTERVIEWS

Interviews are analyzed to determine stakeholder views on the questions asked and to identify other concerns/issues that emerged in the course of the interviews. The intent is to objectively and systematically identify specified characteristics of the messages of the stakeholders (Holsti, 1969). This process involves identifying categories of response and summarizing these by interviewer group. The summary is used in a later step to contrast stakeholder perceptions and to draw conclusions for recommendations on program changes and/or evaluation plans.

The act of summarizing means that some data will be omitted. There is a tendency for some summarizers (and some reviewers) to assign importance to a stakeholder view (and thus make a decision about inclusion in the summary) by reference to the number expressing the view. However, in evaluability assessment a view may be vital if only one stakeholder expresses it because of that individual's special perspective or degree of insight.

> ...what one individual experiences is not necessarily unreliable, biased, or a matter of opinion, just as what a number of individuals experience is not necessarily reliable, factual, and confirmable. ...Depending upon the qualities, training, and experience of the (person), his reports may be more factual and confirmable than the reports of a group. (Guba and Lincoln, 1981, p. 125)

In other words, the number of times a stakeholder mentions something in a structured interview is not as significant as the fact that it was mentioned; a skilled interviewer will keep the discussion moving to capture as much different information on the questions as is possible within the time allowed.

Patton (1980) noted that analyzing qualitative data--which interviews from EAs are--is a creative process and may be approached in different ways by different people. It is based more on a researcher's experience and knowledge of a particular subject than on tried and true analysis methods. And, most reports of qualitative studies describe the results without explaining the analysis process. This is done intentionally by some authors who believe that each research situation, with different materials to analyze and different research objectives, requires different techniques. For example, Markoff et al. (1975) take this position and indicate that no prescription can or should be offered. This causes problems for the inexperienced researcher who plans qualitative studies without realizing the work involved; it prevents replication of studies; and it slows down the development of a set of workable procedures.

The Markoff et al. (1975) position is not advocated here. There may be NO ONE model or approach that is universally applicable but what has worked in one instance may work in another and/or stimulate thoughts about how to proceed.

There are similarities to the functions of qualitative data analysis just as there are to quantitative; there are certain problems which must be resolved, regardless of the content area and the objectives. Norris (1981) listed five of these problems as managing the volume of data, devising a conceptual scheme, incorporating the data into that scheme, establishing reliability, and establishing validity. Narayanan (1987) described procedures for managing these problems with specific guidelines for handling and processing data, reducing the data, displaying and interpreting the data, and drawing conclusions and verifying.

The first three sections of Narayanan's procedures are summarized below. These are all that are required for describing and differentiating stakeholder views. (Drawing conclusions and making recommendations is a separate and later EA step.) These procedural steps are followed by descriptions of the techniques used in the Extension EAs. For the most part, these are techniques which emerged to fit the situations and conditions of the individual EAs. That was not by design. As indicated earlier, there are few detailed illustrations of procedures and techniques for performing content analysis (especially on semi-structured interview data), and the Narayanan work was not yet available. In fact, his work originated as a result of need identified in carrying out the first three CES EAs!

The procedures presented below may not all be necessary for every person conducting EAs. The formality with which each procedure is carried out will depend upon the experience of the person collecting and analyzing the data, the availability of resources, the number of interviewers, the importance of the study, and its scope. Persons who are experienced in using qualitative data may not need to implement all the steps in a formal detailed manner. They will, however, have to deal with the major steps in some fashion, i.e., processing, summarizing, and presenting the data so it can be understood.

Full transcriptions of interviews may be unnecessary where one person is conducting all the interviews. When more than one interviewer is used, full transcriptions or very detailed write-ups of completed interviews can be very important. In the Maryland 4-H study, recorded tapes and handwritten summaries were provided by the interviewer assisting the EA director (who conducted some of the interviews, herself). After listening to a sample of the tapes and comparing them to the handwritten notes, the EA was held up until full transcriptions could be made of all the interviews conducted by the other person. The handwritten notes contained what the interviewer thought was important but they omitted much of the rich detail that was used to support the study conclusions.

Detailed coding may be unnecessary where full transcriptions are available and the number of interviews is not too extensive. The person analyzing the data can read and reread the interviews and identify evaluator positions.

For very important studies, for large studies, and for studies conducted by persons who are inexperienced in qualitative data gathering and analysis, the different steps should be followed. If the study is sensitive, having the interviews fully transcribed can be insurance for the report writer--doubtful persons can be provided copies of pertinent transcripts. If the study is very large, identifying categories and assigning codes for computer sorting and retrieval may be necessary to capture the important points from each interview. And, if the data analyzer is a novice where qualitative data are concerned, implementing all the steps will help insure that important stakeholder views are not lost; also, going through the whole process a few times, will move the novice out of that experiential level! The steps can be structured in the following array.

Data Handling and Processing

1. Transcribe and/or write up completed interviews. Save interviewer comments and observations even though verbatim transcriptions may be made.

2. Place each interview in a separate file. Maintain duplicates whether as hard copy or computer diskettes. Keep a master copy that is <u>never</u> used--always work from copies.

3. Edit texts. In editing, three questions are considered: (a) Is the transcription accurate? (b) Are meanings conveyed

clearly? and (c) Is each segment relevant to inquiry? Be careful to NOT impose meaning where none exists or where the respondent has given an ambiguous response. Note evidence of bias expressed or implied by the interviewer or the respondent. Identify seemingly irrelevant material but do not discard it--meaning may later emerge.

Reducing the Data

1. Identify categories and develop codes. Read and reread interviews to locate and identify specific information which addresses the relevant questions and issues. Code segments in the margins using some system of letters and/or numbers or key words. Make these short and easily recognizable--especially if computer retrieval is intended.

2. Refine and apply the system of codes. More categories (and codes) may be identified than are finally used. Follow a cumulative process: new categories are added as new information is obtained; at the same time, previously defined categories may be changed to include nuances that become apparent from new information. Changes in codes at any point require previously coded interviews to be checked and recoded as necessary.

3. Validate coding system and its application. Have different persons code the same interviews and check for differences. Such differences can reveal misinterpretations of respondent intent, omission of relevant passages, and ambiguous codes. Make sure clean transcripts, without codes and underlinings, are provided for the verifiers.

Displaying Data

1. Cluster the codes into categories which address similar issues. Previous steps have dealt with single segments of information, clustering juxtaposes these segments and relates one to the other. Continue grouping and regrouping until it is possible to clearly identify the main themes expressed by respondents.

2. Display the categories. Narayanan (1987) discusses a number of techniques for displaying data, e.g., dendrograms, summary tables, matrix displays, and flow charts. Though all of these may be helpful to some extent, the summary table is the most useful. The simplest kind of summary table gives the number of responses in each category for each question asked or each aspect covered. Illustrations from the interview texts may be placed alongside the numbers for each category, to give a feeling for the kinds of information collected. These tables provide an idea of the range of the study, the number and categories of respondents who have been interviewed, and the response rates for each subdivision of information.

EXAMPLES FROM CES CASE STUDIES

The master gardener study in California and the one on public officials in Illinois were carried out simultaneously and followed the same procedure:

1. Personal interviews were conducted and transcriptions made by interviewers from handwritten notes. Illinois interviewees subsequently verified accuracy of transcripts.
2. Three copies were made of each interview. Two work group members each received a copy and one copy was given to the EA consultant. Originals were maintained in a separate file.
3. Each interview was read and reread to get some sense of the content and context of the interviewee responses.
4. Response units were handwritten on 3 x 5 index cards with a different color for each predetermined category, e.g., green cards for program effects, blue for concerns, etc. Each card contained only one unit, e.g., one concern or one effect, and each was coded so the interviewee, the stakeholder group, and the analyzer could be identified. No attempt was made to limit units or categories. Any responses which seemed pertinent but did not fit the predetermined categories (the

structured questions) were written on white cards and coded by the reader.

5. After all response units were recorded, the cards were stacked in piles by color. Each stack was sorted by a member of the task group. A tentative decision was made on each card as to whether it belonged to the category. Those that did not seem to fit a color were placed in the white "miscellaneous" pile.

6. Seemingly duplicate responses were paper clipped together. (Note that duplicates were anticipated since each interview was analyzed by at least two persons.) Where "duplicates" were interpreted the same by both analyzers, one card was discarded. Where there were differences, the two reader-analyzers referred back to the interview and reached agreement. Sometimes this resulted in both cards being kept, meaning that two thoughts were conveyed rather than one.

7. The miscellaneous stack was sorted in similar fashion to the others.

8. After sorting was completed, all cards in a category were arranged on a table so that all units were viewable.

9. Group discussion then followed about each category.

10. These were later typed but most of the analysis occurred at that one setting.

In the Maryland 4-H study, the procedure used was very similar to that suggested by Smith and Lincoln (1984). One person analyzed all the interviews, summarized them by category by stakeholder group, and then verified the summary with the EA task group. The steps were as follows:

1. Personal interviews were conducted and transcriptions made from electronic recordings.

2. One copy was made and the original filed.

3. Interviews were separated by stakeholder group and coded by group and by person, e.g., III-A could be the elected officials group and the person interviewed, the Secretary of the Department of Agriculture.

4. Interviews were read several times to get a general sense of the content.

5. Sections were marked and codes written in margins. Codes were identified for the questions and for emerging categories. For example, though no question was asked about implementing 4-H through schools, several persons identified some aspect of that as a concern. Similarly, some persons made comments about competition in 4-H events. Notations in the margins to identify these two emerging categories were as follows: III-A Schools (-), I-B Schools (+), III-C Competition (-), IV-B Competition (+). The (+ 's) and (-'s) following the descriptions made it easier later on to categorize by affective direction of stakeholder response (positive, negative) as well as by content. (For example, "III-A Schools (-)" meant the interviewee was person A in stakeholder group III who made a comment about 4-H in the schools and the comment was negative.)

6. A running list of categories was kept and tentatively clustered.

7. Pages were cut and separated by category.

8. All quotes for a category were taped consecutively on sheets of paper.

9. Similar comments were counted and arranged in listings. For example, one stakeholder group (volunteers) perceived the mission of 4-H as being to
   -teach life skills (4)
   -develop/create better, more responsible citizens (3)
   -etc.
   Numbers in parentheses indicate number of volunteers providing the same response.

10. Summaries were written for each stakeholder group for each category. Responses were described as succinctly as possible without losing or destroying the naturalness of the data.

11. The EA task group was convened; each member was given a copy of all the interviews for one group of stakeholders. Members read interviews once or twice, making notes in margins as desired. They read until they felt some sense of what that group was saying. Stakeholder group summaries were then provided and task group members checked these against their notes

and the verbatim interviews to identify omissions, commissions, questionable interpretations, etc.
12. Differences were discussed and reconciled and a "group consensus" summary prepared.

COMPUTERIZED CODING

Computerized text coding can be used to locate, count, and tabulate specified characteristics of texts. This process has the advantages of reliability, speed, and coder labor savings. Earlier versions of this type of software restricted content analysis to characteristics of texts, e.g., word frequencies, and required fully operationalized criteria in advance of doing the counts (Woodrum, 1984). Ideas and concepts requiring full sentences and those which were contextually bound were likely to be missed. Later versions of text-manipulating software have vastly improved capabilities and are highly recommended for EAs where very many and/or very long interviews are recorded. Machine coding was not used in the CES EAs because of the lack of availability of computer capability at the different sites.

Two microcomputer programs useful for analyzing textual data which have been successfully used with open-ended interviews are ASKSAM (1986) and FYI 3000 Plus (1987). Individual blocks of text, e.g., a few words, sentences, paragraph, etc., can be marked (coded) much as one would manually identify and name important passages on a page of typed print. Once all the pages are coded, an automatic search can be made to count all occurrences of a particular code and/or generate a separate file containing all marked blocks of text where a coded passage occurred, across all interviews. A sorted file can be subcoded for finer distinctions and nuances of the data.

· · · · ·

The product from this step is a summary of stakeholder views on each question and on any other categories that emerged. The format and formality of this product may differ depending on such factors as the competencies of the analyzer, the scope of the study, and the needs of stakeholders. At the least, though, it should accurately present the essence of the data and differences among stakeholder groups.

CHAPTER NINE

Identify Stakeholder Needs, Concerns, and Differences in Perceptions

The purpose of this task is to identify both common understandings and major differences among stakeholders in their perceptions about what a program is trying to accomplish and how it is being implemented.

The steps for each question in this section are (1) compare stakeholder perceptions of the program with the program model, (2) validate any differences with more data, e.g., reinterviews, and (3) report findings to the primary EA client and/or other primary evaluation users.

IS THERE AGREEMENT IN GENERAL ABOUT THE OVERALL INTENT OF THE PROGRAM?

Comparisons should be made among key stakeholder group perceptions and program outcomes as depicted on the final portions of the If-Then logic model. If these are congruent, the next question can be addressed.

When differences appear, the first step is to determine
if:
  a. the key stakeholder* expectations represent reality but
     accidently got omitted from the program model, or
  b. the key stakeholder expectations are not presently being
     planned or implemented but the program staff agree
     they should be, or
  c. the key stakeholder expectations are considered
     unrealistic by the staff.

The first two situations present no problems if staff have
or can generate activities and resources to support the
expectations.   Disagreement about inclusion (c) can be a
problem.   When that occurs, critical stakeholders should be
contacted--but not until staff have clarified the basis for their
disagreement.
Stakeholder recontacts will be handled differently
depending on the importance of the stakeholder and the
amount of influence he/she can wield on the program. If the
person/group is not too critical to the program, explanations
can be provided for why their expectations are not being
fulfilled. If the stakeholders can have great impact on the
program, they definitely should be asked about the importance
of the goal/objective and given the staff reservations. If there
is still disagreement, the person(s) ultimately responsible for
the program may engage in a negotiated process to arrive at a
solution and/or may look to the EA leader/evaluator for some
direction about what is the more reasonable course to pursue.
Through negotiation and agreement or selection efforts, a final
decision is made.
It is hard to imagine an impasse developing among
persons knowledgeable about a program. Unfortunately, what
is more likely is that the expectation will be embraced "on
paper" and then no action taken to make it happen. No visible
harm will result until an evaluation is conducted to determine
if the event was carried out and/or if it had the planned effect.
In none of the CES EAs did differences emerge between
stakeholder expectations and program actions that were major

---

* Key stakeholders, as specified here, are very influential persons who are not
members of the program implementation staff.

enough to recontact the stakeholders. Such differences have occurred in prior evaluations as the following two examples show.

In the first example, key influentials of a CES small farms program thought the program should aim to increase the net income of farmers. Program staff felt net income was too much outside their control (for reasons like weather, interest rates, inflation, etc.) and instead chose the goal "to improve farmer production efficiency and effectiveness." The initial goal, "increased net income," was measurable in net dollar increase from a previous year; the later goal, "efficiency/effectiveness" could be estimated from practices adopted by the farmers and in some instances, verified by farmer records. The latter goal was more within their purview to influence. Once the key influentials were appraised of the logic of this goal change, they withdrew their objections.

The second example was where key influentials expected a nutrition program to educate and motivate people to change their health practices and lead healthier lifestyles, e.g., reduce fats in their diets, reduce cholesterol, increase exercise. The program developer had planned the program to impart knowledge, e.g., participants would learn nutritional values in foods. In this instance the program developer changed the program; activities were planned to encourage practice change, and ways were identified to determine if they did, in fact, occur.

IS THERE AGREEMENT ABOUT WHO IS TO BE SERVED BY THE PROGRAM?

This question may have already been answered with the data on intent. The concern is about the number and type of targeted audience. For example, should the 4-H program serve rural and/or urban youth? Should the home-based business program work with present owners and/or help new persons get started? Should the program serve the traditional home economics industries like a seamstress operation or should it serve any type of home-based business owner? Any major discrepancy should be handled the same as for previous questions. If such questions are not clear prior to an impact evaluation, stakeholders may be very unhappy with a program's results even though it did accomplish what was intended.

In the Maryland 4-H study, program staff listed volunteers as an intended audience of the program. Several other stakeholder groups did not; they saw volunteers as deliverers of the program. If an impact study were conducted on the program showing definite effects for/on volunteers, it is quite likely that stakeholders would not be impressed <u>unless</u> positive gains were <u>also</u> shown for youth--the audience they felt the program should benefit.

IS THERE AGREEMENT ABOUT SUPPORT ACTIVITIES AND/OR RESOURCES?

Many stakeholders will not have enough detailed information on a program to question specific activities that are implemented to bring about intended results. Differences that do occur, if they are really significant, should be handled in the same way as with the previous questions, i.e., reconciled by program staff and key stakeholders. Examples of types of differences in expectations that could occur in CES programs are that the 4-H agent would attend community club meetings; or that the aquaculture agent would assist with the physical work of pond drainage and/or fish harvesting; or that a home-based-business agent would make home visits; etc.

The question of resources is different. Key stakeholders will usually have definite perceptions about resources. Whereas some may not be very concerned about what activities are implemented as long as they promote the intended effect, they do care about the amount of resources used. In the plausibility analysis, program staff may have reached the conclusion that resources are insufficient to achieve all the goals. Higher-level internal and key external stakeholders, on the other hand, may feel they are adequate and that the program should continue working toward all its objectives with no resources added.

Any disagreement on resources will be harder to deal with than the previous questions because the arguments for both sides may include less concrete evidence. One reason is that resources in many agencies are not assigned on a specific program basis--except in broad categories--and thus are difficult to track on this basis. The amount of resources spent on a particular program will vary based on staff interest and/or competency in the area, staff directedness--reactive or proactive--and the individual area needs.

A second reason that adequacy of resources can be elusive is that it depends if one thinks of adequacy in terms of what is being done or in terms of what someone thinks is needed to be done. For example, the resources might be perceived as adequate for meeting the needs of the number of youth presently in a 4-H program or the number of clients reached in a drug rehabilitation program but inadequate to reach the number the staff would like to reach.

An answer also depends on how resources are being used. If intended effects are not being achieved by a program, it could be that resources are being expended on the wrong activities or that the activities are being implemented poorly. An EA does not measure achievement of program effects but it can provide evidence about "wrong" activities--when the program model's plausibility is questioned--and may provide some evidence on quality of implementation--through stakeholder concerns expressed in interviews.

Any or all of the three areas examined here--program intent, audience served, and support activities and resources-- are legitimate issues for an intensive followup evaluation, if stakeholder interest warrants. The very act of raising these questions in the EA may create stakeholder need/desire to know, over and beyond other questions that are surfaced in the initial interviews.

DEFINE STAKEHOLDER EVALUATION NEEDS

To this point the EA has provided one of its intended primary outcomes--a fully described and plausible program with elements logically linked and well defined. Or, evidence has been provided that such a program does not exist! Or, evidence shows a partially described and plausible program with areas that need further articulation. The second primary outcome has also been achieved with the exception of one part--clarification of stakeholder needs for evaluative information on the program.

The achievement of the first outcome--defined program theory--will already have answered some stakeholder inquiries. Some of them will simply want to know that a program is goal oriented, that its goals are clear and not contrary to what they see as important. Others may not specify evaluation needs but may talk about what they see as important in the program. These are tips for the program leader. S/He may pick up cues for future information needs. In other words, there will be some stakeholders who want to know specific things about a program, there will be others who do not verbalize concerns but would be impressed with certain findings.

What stakeholders want to know about a program can be almost as varied as the stakeholders themselves, and the positions they occupy relative to the program may not be good predictors. For example, funders, program managers, and persons in political offices may each be interested in accountability concerns, e.g., goal achievement, who the program reaches and does not, and how many it reaches; all three may also be interested in knowing about individual success cases and other information that can help them answer constituent complaints, and make appropriate alterations in resource allocations. Other interests like program improvement, implementation adequacy, quality control, quality assurance, and program expansion, to name a few, may be equally cross cutting.

If their informational interests/needs could be neatly categorized, there would be little reason for interviews to be conducted. Data could be collected, analyzed, and presented at leisurely intervals. Since that is not the case, the purpose of this step is to identify who wants to know what about a program and to determine what will best satisfy their informational needs. The product should be a list of evaluation concerns prioritized on the basis of the importance of the stakeholder(s) desiring the information, available resources, and the potential for impact of the data on program and/or personnel. It may not be desirable or feasible to address all evaluation concerns. Where there is a tradeoff, examination of a few issues in depth may provide the most positive and lasting impact.

CHAPTER TEN

Determine Plausibility of Program Model

Expectations are plausible "when there is some evidence that the program activity on site will achieve the results expected, and there is no evidence to the contrary" (Schmidt et al., 1979, pp. 50-51). Basically, the plausibility question asks if necessary and sufficient conditions exist for a program to succeed. These conditions exist for a program if:

1. it intends to bring about some change,
2. its intentions are clear,
3. its planned activities are reasonable, i.e., they are of the right nature to influence the expected outcome,
4. its activities are sufficient in quantity and quality to exert that influence,
5. its resources are present in sufficient amount and type for the activities to be implemented as planned.

Four questions are answered in this exercise to determine plausibility: Are overall program goals well defined? Are the different parts of the program well defined? Are the activities sufficient in type and amount? and, Are resources adequate to implement the activities? EA can answer the first two questions better than it can the latter two and can answer all four better when there are obvious omissions or lacks. In other words, a full scale evaluation to measure goal attainment will be necessary to know for sure if the resources are adequate and if the activities are sufficient. However, an EA can provide a reasonable estimation of the likelihood of different parts of the program achieving intended goals and of identified resources being adequate to implement the different parts. An EA can reduce uncertainty about adequacy and plausibility and prevent futile evaluations where goals are "obviously" implausible.

Much of the information for answering these questions will come from the program model described and validated by program staff. However, some very important data may come from stakeholder interviews. Therefore, before reviewing the program description for plausibility, the team should make sure it has a thorough understanding of stakeholder views. Their concerns may alert reviewers to aspects of the program where more careful scrutiny is required than might otherwise be thought necessary.

ARE OVERALL GOALS WELL DEFINED?

Goals are well defined and measurable if they:

1. are clearly stated,
2. have identifiable indicators of successful performance (criteria and standards), and
3. have identifiable sources to provide evidence of performance

ARE COMPONENTS/ACTIVITIES WELL DEFINED?

A component is well defined and measurable if it has:

1. a known purpose (clear objective),
2. identifiable supporting activities,
3. identifiable resources for the activities,
4. identifiable indicators of successful performance (criteria and standards), and

5. identifiable sources that can provide evidence of performance.

ARE COMPONENTS/ACTIVITIES SUFFICIENT?

Sufficiency is a condition for an individual component and for the total program. A program can have several components that, in and of themselves, are sufficient but if one is critical and it is not sufficient to achieve its purpose, then the program will lack plausibility.

To be sufficient, activities must be defined and of the type, quality, and quantity needed to bring about the desired purpose. "...of the type needed" means there is reason to believe the activities lead to certain outcomes. Some questions that may be asked are:

1. Is the content broad enough?
2. Is there enough information for the client to learn or do what is proposed?
3. Even if the clients learned (whatever concept/task), what else must they know or what else must they have (equipment, services, other resources) to make the planned changes?
4. Can the client acquire sufficient skill to perform the practice with the amount of planned contact with the program?
5. What evidence is there that clients already know (a necessary prerequisite) before they come to the program?
6. Has consideration been given to actions clients must take, e.g., how to get them to provide realistic and private-in-nature data required for assistance with financial analysis?
7. Is it clear what others (besides clients) must do to insure the success of the events, e.g., other agencies?
8. Are strategies identified to involve key influentials for program legitimation?
9. Are promotional efforts consistent with and pertinent to the targeted audience?

ARE RESOURCES ADEQUATE?

Questions to ask to determine adequacy of resources include:

1. Are resources clearly identified as to type and amount needed? For example, qualification and number of staff, experts, and other resource personnel; the number and type of teaching materials, equipment, facilities.
2. Are the resources available? For example, in CES programs, is state specialist support available in the needed area? Have materials been developed or will they be by implementation time?
3. Given other system "have-to's" is it likely the resources will be allotted to the program as needed?

To answer these four sets of questions about plausibility requires a clear definition of what is needed and what is in place, and then deciding if there is a good match between the two. Social science theory, research, expert opinion, and previous program evaluations are all good sources for evidence of plausibility. But, some of the best evidence may come from stakeholder interviews, especially their concerns about the program.

Gaps may show up. One reason is that programs are often started as no more than statements of intent, e.g., improve nutritional status of young children, when how to intervene and what to expect from the interventions are unclear. A second reason is that in the past we have not kept very good records of what we did and what, if any, difference it made. (When resources were abundant, we did not have to keep such records!) A third reason is that many, many activities are planned and implemented without prior expectations for specific performance--without thinking through how the activity should affect another activity and/or clients. When the end result is not clear--at least as far as intent is concerned--there is no way to know what to measure to know if it has been reached.

In the final analysis, plausibility is pretty much a judgment call and it is much easier to make in cases where obvious gaps exist in planning and/or in the implementation. The more usual case though is where "something" is planned or in place and the question is one of sufficiency. This can be a difficult process if staff are made to feel threatened. Allowing them to go through the analysis and arriving at their own conclusions about plausibility will be easier for all concerned, and the EA will already have done some good.

One method for taking some of the judgment out of the plausibility conclusion and acquiring "concrete" criteria is to have the staff outline their assumptions about (1) the problem solving process participants must go through to achieve program goals, and (2) what will motivate participants to want to go through that problem solving process. These are modeled sequentially and causally much like the logic of the program is described. Then, when the model of program implementation is produced, the components and activities can be examined to determine sufficiency in content and motivational aspects. Staff can look at what they said is required (problem-solving model) and compare that to what is ongoing or planned (program theory model).

When the goal of the EA is to plan a program, the question is one of plausibility of intent. When the program is ongoing, the question is plausibility of action. Either way, outlining their basic assumptions about client action and motivation provides a point of comparison.

This procedure was created as a part of the fourth EA-- for the Oklahoma home-based-business program. The goal of that EA was to plan a plausible program. So, the question was on what basis would plausibility of intent be judged. Figure 10-1 shows the problem solving model that was assumed for the participants; Table 10-1 lists the assumptions about motivators. In the planning mode, these two exercises are used to plan content and delivery mechanisms to cover each assumption. Anticipated activities are referenced to key events and motivators. This makes it easy to see where gaps exist and where there is overlap.

Stakeholder interviews can also provide strong evidence for program plausibility. As an example, one component in the Maryland 4-H logic model is "Agents and Volunteers Train Volunteers." The purpose is "to orient volunteers to 4-H and

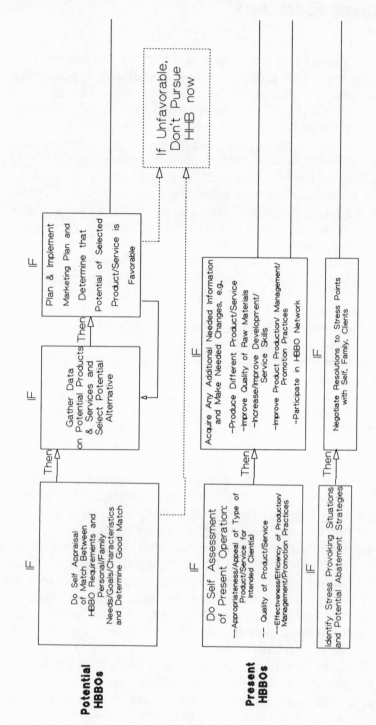

Figure 10-1. Home-based business CES program. (Smith 1988.)

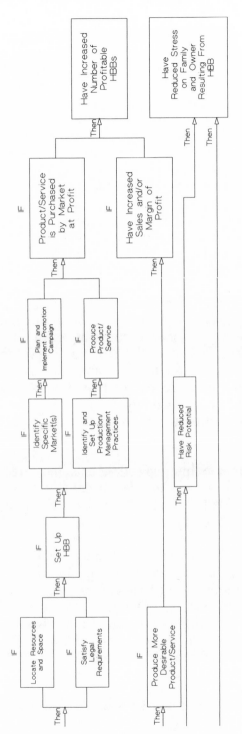

Figure 10-1. Continued.

the CES and to prepare them to work with youth to achieve desired program effects." The conclusion was reached that the plausibility of this component was "questionable" in terms of enabling youth to achieve the effects known as life skills. Data from stakeholder interviews were used to support this conclusion. Excerpts from the EA report show the evidence:*

> According to interviewed county faculty, the activities identified for training volunteers represent the ideal. They indicate that no one county is probably implementing all the activities, and some may be doing very few. Each of the agents making input was doing some of them. (p. 17)

> Part of the reason for this discrepancy is that the number and types of volunteers differ from county to county as does the extent and formality of the training. There is no specified curriculum for training volunteers and county and state faculty, and the volunteers themselves, say they are not getting the training and guidance they need. County faculty also say many volunteers will not participate when training is offered. (p. 17)

> None of the nine interviewed agents indicated that his/her leader training identified or defined the specific effects (life skills) that youth are supposed to develop/refine. (p. 18)

> The twelve volunteers who were interviewed...were not asked questions about their training. However, three mentioned training when asked if they had any implementation concerns. One said "4-H loses leaders because they just get overwhelmed and discouraged." Another said she had never been told what she was expected to do and that she needed help. (p. 20)

---

*See Appendix Two for more detail on 4-H program plausibility.

The volunteer from "X" County said he did <u>not</u> receive training or suggestions from CES on how to teach life skills. (p. 20)

Evidence from stakeholders is not always so obvious, thus the concrete criteria, up front, of staff assumptions is desirable to be included.

In the evaluability assessments conducted by CES the plausibility question lost some significance because as the staff saw weaknesses in program logic as the program was being described, they made changes right then and there. For example, one program person in the Illinois EA made a comment like "How can we expect (a key component) to happen with just that one activity? Don't you (other program staff) think we could do..." and she suggested some activities they had the resources to do. After some discussion, the staff agreed on a set of activities to support the intended impact and these became a part of the program model.

Even though it is clear that the final call on plausibility can be determined only after the program has been implemented and sufficient time has elapsed for the intended change(s) to occur, best estimations can be made. If these are made on the basis of criteria presented in this chapter with evidence collected and analyzed as suggested in previous chapters, resources may be saved and/or the program changed to better serve its intended clientele.

Table 10-1.   Participant Motivators, Oklahoma Home-based
                     Business Program.

To want to change, the participant must:

o   Expect to receive something desired,
o   Expect a return greater than the expected risk,
o   Expect to be successful--to not fail,
o   Perceive the effort as not too hard,
o   See the effort as compatible with "self"--don't have to stretch
       too much,
o   Understand the totality of the effort--see what is required,
o   Have ability to change--knowledge and resources, and
o   Believe someone else cares.

CHAPTER ELEVEN

Draw Conclusions
and
Make Recommendations

Within the evaluation field, questions about conclusions and recommendations range from "Should they be made?" to "How can they be justified?" Answers to these questions differ depending on the purpose of the study, the type(s) of data on which conclusions are based, who is making them, and who they are made for.

SHOULD CONCLUSIONS BE DRAWN AND RECOMMENDATIONS MADE?

The answer to this question is obvious by the presence of this chapter--of course they should be made. It is hard to imagine responsible individuals studying a program or issue over an extended period of time and not having some insights to share. Also, is that not the reason for studying a program-- to be able to draw conclusions about the way it has or is functioning?

In reality, the drawing of conclusions is not a next-to-last step, as presented in this text. It is a continuing process throughout the EA. For example, in the development/ clarification of program theory (Step 4), conclusions are drawn about what is and is not a part of the program; in Step 7, conclusions are drawn about stakeholder perceptions of the program; and Step 8, on plausibility, requires conclusions about adequacy of activities, resources, and performance indicators. What is different at this step, is looking at the whole EA process and saying "What did we learn? and What should we do about it?"

WHO SHOULD DRAW CONCLUSIONS AND MAKE RECOMMENDATIONS

Prominent evaluation theorists disagree about the appropriateness of evaluators drawing conclusions and making recommendations for program changes (House, 1986; Scriven, 1985). House is generally "for," but says there are circumstances that warrant not doing so; Scriven is "for" and somewhat "against"--for drawing conclusions and somewhat against making recommendations. Scriven (1985) is of the opinion that bad things should be labeled bad and good things labeled good even if one does not know why they are that way. He notes that making recommendations may go beyond evaluator competence into the realm of subject-matter expertise and therefore be more in the purview of program staff. Smith (J.K., 1987) offers another perspective about the evaluator drawing conclusions and that is the risk involved: evaluators do not have the same degree of involvement, or as much at risk, as do program staff; the former, whether internal or external, can usually go on to other things while the latter must live with whatever decisions are made.

Scriven's concern about evaluators stepping outside their realm of competence is not a worry in EAs implemented as discussed here and as was done in the Extension studies. Program staff are involved in every step of the process, including deciding what conclusions are warranted, based on the data, and what recommendations can be justified, based on the conclusions and the program. For example, they help define criteria for program plausibility and summarize stakeholder views and identify differences among stakeholder groups, all before being involved in recommending next steps.

WHAT SHOULD CONCLUSIONS AND RECOMMENDATIONS BE MADE ABOUT?

Conclusions should cover whatever questions were asked and anything else of significance that emerged from the study. For example, if the EA was a prelude to an impact study and/or if it was done for program improvement purposes, some of the questions would be: Is there general agreement among influential stakeholders about the intent of the program--mission, goals, intended audience, intended effects, resources? What, if any, major concerns were identified about how the program is functioning--from stakeholder perspectives and/or from theory plausibility? If the EA was conducted in the planning mode, the first question could be asked if stakeholders beyond program staff were interviewed. Otherwise, conclusions would be drawn about some one or more persons' assessments of plausibility of the program if it were implemented as described on paper. In reality, this would be conclusions about the rhetoric about the program. Only after the program is implemented can attempts be made to reconcile rhetoric with reality. Once conclusions are drawn, recommendations should then describe action targeted to overcome any deficits, weaknesses, concerns.

HOW CAN CONCLUSIONS AND RECOMMENDATIONS BE JUSTIFIED?

Justifying conclusions is one of the most problematic issues facing all types of evaluation (Smith, J. K., 1987). What are the guidelines for sorting, emphasizing, classifying, and resolving characteristic perspectives within and on an evaluation study (Pearsol, 1987)? What are the types of claims (question-answer propositions) whose justification is of interest (Smith, N., 1987)? What information brokering requirements must be met (McClintock, 1987)? On the basis of what evidence and criteria are conclusions justified (Greene, 1987a)? How can one use his/her skills of persuasion and analysis to mediate among the different perspectives to select evidence and claims for conclusions (Pearsol, 1987)? What constitutes legitimate knowledge about a program or issue (Farley, 1987)?

These are questions asked about naturalistic evaluations in a special section of Volume 10, Number 4, of Evaluation and Program Planning. Even though EAs are not naturalistic evaluations, they do generate qualitative data and thus are vulnerable to some of the same validity and reliability threats. There is not space or reason to deal with all those questions here. It is important, though, to examine why anyone should believe in the results from an evaluability assessment. This rationale is important in the very first step of an EA in securing commitment of key stakeholders to the process, later in securing commitment from the persons who describe their program theory, and in the final step in convincing those same stakeholders to act on the results.

The concepts of validity and reliability are understood somewhat differently for qualitative and quantitative data--at least they are understood differently by those espousing the naturalistic/qualitative approaches! These differences have been discussed in detail by others including Bredo and Feinberg, 1982; Guba and Lincoln, 1981; and House, 1980 (Pearsol, 1987). The intent here is not to defend one position or the other. However, in presentations on EA to different groups, many of whom have been hard science researchers who were also engaged in extension work, questions about credibility and validity have arisen and they were worded in the quantitative context. These questions have been "answered" by describing the type(s) of data generated by an EA and offering reasons certain potentially biasing situations seem not to be threats to an EA. Discussion of these points follows.

EVALUABILITY ASSESSMENT DATA

Data collected for an EA are mostly qualitative and primarily perceptual in nature. Qualitative data are "natural" reports of experience and as such can be very beneficial for identifying unique impacts of a program (Smith and Lincoln, 1984). They are used to provide insight into unique experiences of respondents or aspects of settings. They are generally perceived to yield more indepth information about a smaller number of units than do directly quantifiable data.

Many in the research arena believe qualitative data are less valid than quantitative. However, a fundamental oversight by this group has been to misinterpret quantifications as replacing rather than depending upon ordinary perception and judgment. Sir Josiah Stamp knew this when he said:

> The Government is very keen on amassing statistics. They collect them, add them, raise them to the nth power, take the cube root and prepare wonderful diagrams. But you must never forget that every one of these figures comes in the first instance from the village watchman, who just puts down what he pleases (Evaluation News, 1985, p.44).

Perceptual data are those conceptions or beliefs about reality as understood by a person's senses. They may or may not represent "truth" as concrete, objective data would show a situation to be. However, the first point that communications researchers make is that "objective" reality does not exist (Rocheleau, 1986). Drucker (1967) described executives who make effective decisions as those who know that one does not start with facts but with opinions. John F. Kennedy was believed to act on this basis (Halberstam, 1979):

> He (Kennedy) put, aides noticed, more concentration into watching the news than into almost anything else. ...Perhaps it was not reality...not even good journalism, but it was what the country perceived as reality and thus in a way was closer to reality than reality itself (p. 388).

The effectiveness of many types of programs, including those of CES, is often not directly verifiable (Edelman, 1977). And, even those programs that lend themselves to "objective" assessments may not be successful in translating that effectiveness/efficiency to public "knowledge." Nimmo and Combs (1983) note that "knowledge" requires a depth of understanding about a program including a grasp of complexities and relationships. Rocheleau (1986) said the public is not interested nor capable of keeping abreast of the latest findings concerning a program's effectiveness. He quoted a staff member to the Senate Labor and Human Resources Committee commenting about a public program which had research to show effectiveness:

> Asked whether she thought the current service delivery system had to be changed because it didn't work, Higgins said that many "perceived" that the current system was a failure, and in politics, "perception is reality" (emphasis added). (p. 831)

The point here is that arguments may be offered pro and con about the validity of types of data collected in an EA --qualitative and perceptual. However, if a program's public has a belief about that program, it will act on the basis of that belief. Thus, the uncovering of negative perceptions requires programmatic action whether the perceptions are true or false. If they are true, the program will need to change (take action) if the public's beliefs about it are to change. If they are false, the program will need to correct the public's perceptions (take action).

POTENTIAL VALIDITY THREATS

Cook and Campbell (1979) point out that data can never be completely free of bias, that "causal inferences will never be proved with certainty since the inferences we make depend upon many assumptions that cannot be directly verified" (p. 94). Qualitative and quantitative data are open to validity threats such as observer bias, however, it is not the type of data that is collected which determines credibility of a study but rather how the data are collected and conclusions drawn (and sometimes who draws them).

Some potential validity threats which have surfaced in discussions of EA and which critics might consider most likely are identified with discussion of their probability and impact. These are presented as discussed in quantitative literature because that is how they have surfaced.

1.   Self Report Bias or Evaluation Apprehension:
participants give acceptable responses so as not to appear
inadequate in some way or otherwise intentionally withhold
honest thoughts. This threat is thought to not exist to any great
extent. In the CES studies, interviewees spoke very freely to
all the questions and nearly everyone provided negative and
positive comments. And, since interviewees were asked their
"perceptions" about the program, there were no wrong answers.

2.   Low Statistical Power: present when sample sizes
are too small to yield precise results with high confidence. This
threat does not exist since the intent of evaluability assessment
is not to "prove" findings beyond any shadow of a doubt and
since statistical probability is not attached to conclusions. As
noted earlier, an EA is not equivalent to formal research; its
aim is to inform (Rutman, 1984).   An intent of EA is to
identify areas where program performance is obviously lacking
or at least doubtful and where evaluability is questionable.

3.   Interaction of History and the Treatment: results
when   groups   (individuals)   are   unrepresentative   of   the
populations (groups, programs) to which conclusions are drawn.
This would be the case, for example, if those who provide the
description of the program carry out significantly different
activities than does the average program implementor and/or
if sites chosen for validation are significantly atypical. If this
threat exists, it is believed any bias would be in favor of
showing the program in a more positive light than would be the
case generally--and to lend even greater credibility to any
weaknesses uncovered.   The work group which provides
direction to the EA is usually named by the purchaser of the
EA;   the   persons   providing data for the study--the
stakeholders--are   usually   named   by   the   work   group.
Stakeholders are selected purposefully, each because he/she is
thought to wield a particular influence and to have information
or perceptions about the program in question.

4.   Evaluator/Interviewer Bias: engendered when a
study is subtly shaped to establish a person(s) preconceptions
or desires. This occurs when data are gathered only about

aspects of a program that are suspected to be successful or only about those parts thought to be unsuccessful. It occurs when interviewers "hear" and record only the data that fit their prior beliefs.

The EA process includes efforts to overcome this bias. The aspects of the program to be studied are identified and agreed to by the purchasers of the EA before any data are collected. Also, it is recommended that interviews be conducted by interviewers who have no obvious attachment to the program being studied. If the interviews are recorded, a review of the recorded interviews can reveal any other obvious biasing by the interviewer.

Evaluator bias <u>could be</u> the most troublesome of all the potentially biasing concerns. And, the reading of some writers on naturalistic and qualitative evaluation does not help very much in dealing with the concern. As Smith (J. K., 1987) points out, one could conclude after reading these articles that justifying conclusions is a subjective and rather arbitrary affair. A "fact" that complicates the matter is that objective reality against which to compare conclusions and to adjudicate knowledge claims does not exist (Rocheleau, 1986). There are no "brute data" to appeal to, or *a priori*, neutral criteria to employ to justify conclusions or resolve differences (Smith, J. K., 1987). This does not, however, "release us from the obligation to make the best case possible for our knowledge claims and evaluative conclusions. Moreover, it further obligates us to engage others in free and open dialogue in regard to these claims and conclusions" (Smith, J. K., 1987, p. 354).

Efforts to prevent evaluator bias occur throughout the EA. The work team made up of several members of the program staff are involved in each step. If the stakeholder summary (Step 6) is not produced by them, they read the interview notes/transcriptions and determine that they would describe stakeholder views in the same way or negotiate that final conclusion; if they did not reach the plausibility conclusions, themselves (Step 8), they validate the work of whoever did; and similarly for the other steps.

Inherent in the EA process is an important methodological procedure for increasing trustworthiness of conclusions, i.e., use of multiple data sources. For example, plausibility of the program model for the Maryland 4-H program (Appendix Two) was questioned on the basis of evidence from interviews of several different groups of stakeholders and from gaps in support activities identified for the implemented program model. This triangulation of data made the conclusions more credible than had they been based on a single data source.

GUIDELINES FOR CONCLUSIONS AND RECOMMENDATIONS

1. Do make them.

2. Involve the EA work team, and other potential users where feasible: "...One evaluator's story is just that--one outsider's view of program meaning and significance. ... In contrast, stories about the program--its people and activities, its intents, its worth and meaning--that evolve from shared understandings among the evaluator and multiple evaluation users carry inherent value, defined herein as utility and credibility" (Greene, 1987a, p. 332).

3. Present conclusions with the best reasons possible as to why a situation was read the way it was. Give reasons for recommending a particular course of action over others. Be as accurate as possible but realize that humans make mistakes. Weigh points of view of various sources and forms of evidence; strive for fairness among competing perspectives.

4. Keep personal biases and values out of them as much as possible realizing, of course, that "value neutrality is a state of intellectual life as rare as virginity in sexual life" (Barry and Rae, 1975).

5. Draw conclusions based on evidence from the study; make recommendations based on the study and

knowledge of the implementation scene. Do not over extend on either.

6. Consider the organization's ability/willingness to make changes. Recommendations that are impossible to implement are useless plus they may cast doubt on other aspects of the study.

7. Offer hunches only when asked; only give these verbally; and always label them as such. Some stakeholders do definitely want any perceptions gleaned by the person(s) studying a program. For example, Champion (1985) said he had: "often pleaded with evaluators after their presentations just to go on and give me their unsubstantiated opinion. They have, after all, spent a lot more time looking at a given problem than I, and although they usually haven't been able to come up with a definitive finding on a hard question, they may well have a better feel for a potential answer than I" (p. 39). "...we won't resent a conclusion that goes beyond the evidence so long as you tell us that's what you are offering" (p. 38).

Difficulty in drawing conclusions is increased at the front end of a study by posing unanswerable or unimportant questions and at the back end by not answering the questions that were posed or by answering questions different than the ones posed (N. Smith, 1987). Implementors of EAs, if they follow the advice in this book and all the previous writers on EA, will not have the front end difficulty--their interactions with stakeholders and otherwise careful attention to questions which drive the study will decrease the probability of such problems. These interactions should also help prevent the back-end difficulty--if stakeholders are truly involved as they should be, they will not allow the evaluator to escape without giving attention to agreed-upon front end questions and concerns.

See Appendix Two for conclusions and recommendations which emerged from the Maryland 4-H youth program EA.

CHAPTER TWELVE

Plan Specific Steps for Utilization of EA Data

Planning for utilization is presented here as the last step in carrying out an evaluability assessment but that is not the reality of what should and does happen. Everything done prior to this step is preparing for utilization. Planning for utilization begins when the EA begins, when the purpose of the EA is determined, and continues as each step is implemented. Interestingly enough, evaluability assessment was born to prepare data for use--to learn enough about a program to plan a useful evaluation. And, the CES experience, which was substantiated by Jung and Schubert (1983), has shown that use occurs whether planned or not by conscientious staff who want better, more effective and efficient programs.

The formal action of planning specific steps for using evaluative data--when the decision maker must decide what to do considering the evaluation recommendations and the conditions (constraints, opportunities) of the organization at the time--was judged by Nowakowski (1985) as the toughest part of a study. She notes that one of the difficulties is that recommendations are often worded in terms of the program and not in terms of what is possible for that program in a specific context. However, if, as the previous step suggested, the recommendations have been made interactively with influential stakeholders and/or by or with a program-based work group, this should not be a problem. Both should know, or at least not be off target too much, what the organization's ability is to take action.

There are at least five alternatives for followup to an evaluability assessment, depending on the purpose of the EA:

1. Decide to evaluate the program (or some parts),
2. Decide to change the program.
3. Decide to take no further action.
4. Decide to stop the program.
5. Do not decide, ignore the EA.

If the purpose of the EA is as a prestep to a more intensive study, any one of the alternatives may be chosen. If the purpose of the EA is for program improvement, any one of 2-5 may be chosen. If the purpose is to plan a program, alternatives 2-4 may be chosen but they might be stated a little differently, i.e.:

2. Decide to change the plan.
3. Decide to implement the plan, as is.
4. Decide to not implement the plan.

None of the six CES EAs resulted in the first alternative, i.e., a decision to implement an intensive formative or summative evaluation. Ahead of time it was known the decision was not applicable in two and it quickly became apparent in another. In one of the three where "Decide to evaluate" could have been an appropriate alternative, the program theory model satisfied stakeholder concern about program plausibility (and lead to more resources being provided to the program); in the second, the stakeholders that the staff wanted to influence with evaluative data were not interested; and in the third, alternative 5 happened. Alternative 3 is different from 5 in that the former is a conscious decision to leave things as they are.

This decision not to evaluate in the CES EAs is consistent with Rog's (1985) findings for the 57 EAs she studied. So few of the 57 resulted in followup evaluations that she changed the purpose of her study from that of studying the use of EA followup evaluation results to studying the use of EA results. She did not indicate how many of the 57 actually went on to conduct further evaluation but it was clear that only 45 of the original 57 started off with that intent; only 37 of the 57 EA reports had data on program evaluability (it is not clear that these were 37 of the 45) and of these, 46% of the programs studied were considered "not at all evaluable," 32% had some portion evaluable, and 22% were considered "totally evaluable." These figures suggest that if only a few proceeded with evaluations, the decision makers must have "used" their EA findings appropriately.

In four of the CES EAs, the second alternative--to change the program--was not necessary at the end because changes were made (at least in the espoused program theory and plans) as the EAs ensued. All that was left was to implement the changes. In one of the other two, the Maryland 4-H study, recommendations were made for specific changes and an implementation plan outlined in concert with the administrative leader of the program. In the other, the Maryland water study, the decision has been made to implement on a pilot basis.

These results are not consistent with Rog's (1985) assessment of 57 EAs. She found instrumental use--which is the type of utilization in which program changes would be categorized--to be one of the lowest rated uses for EA results.

These two alternatives for followup--decide to evaluate and decide to change the program--are discussed in more detail below, along with the other three, with suggestions for implementation when each does occur.

1. DECIDE TO EVALUATE

This course of action may be warranted if stakeholder interest in evaluative information is strong and specific, and if the program is evaluable in the area(s) where information interest is focused.

Utilization literature (e.g., Smith, 1988) suggests that use is promoted by stakeholder participation in all phases of the evaluation, including a selection of the methods of inquiry. By this time in the EA, stakeholders will know the evaluation questions that are to be answered and the evaluator will know stakeholders' expected uses for the information. Thus, what is required at this step is the development of the evaluation design. Exactly what is included in the design may vary depending on the evaluation question(s), the evaluator(s), and the stakeholder(s). However, at a minimum, the following seem called for:

o   Statement of evaluation question(s);
o   Anticipated users of the information and estimated uses;
o   Evaluation methods (data to be collected, sources, when, how);
o   Analysis and reporting specifications (products and timeline).

And, whenever possible, stakeholders should be provided alternatives for answering their questions with cost and precision of results estimated for the different approaches. This way, the stakeholder can understand the tradeoffs and make the decisions as to what they will be. For example, the costs of answering a question about an audience with $\pm 5\%$ accuracy (95% confidence) can be three or four times as much as that for $\pm 10\%$: approximately 400 are needed in a sample from a relatively homogeneous population for a precision of $\pm 5\%$ and approximately 100 for $\pm 10\%$ (Smith, 1983; Sudman, 1976). Given this kind of alternative, the purchaser may decide to take the lesser precision rather than scraping the evaluation altogether. Kay (1985) suggested that "confidence level" be thought of in terms of what it would take to convince people to act rather than in terms of statistical probability. That suggestion seems appropriate if the purchaser of information is well acquainted with the requirements and expectations of those s/he wants to influence.

Another element of cost is how much of the data regularly collected by the organization can be analyzed for the current questions. If data collection systems are already in place, e.g., an in-house management information system, then costs will be easy to estimate and probably low. If no data collection system exists, the costs will be higher.

Stakeholders of the CES EAs have been very vague about uses they might have for evaluative information. Comments tended to be general like "to improve the program," and "to show others we are doing a good job." Greene (1987b) reported similar vagueness among stakeholders of two local human service agency evaluations. She reported that these stakeholders would just as soon not be involved in technical evaluation concerns. One of the two evaluation teams in her study did not want to be provided with ratings of technical difficulty (cost) for answering each question nor did they want to identify uses for the results!

Even though stakeholders may choose not to study the evaluation methodology they should be given the opportunity, and official agreements reached between them and the evaluation team. This activity forces the evaluator/evaluation team to think through the strengths and weaknesses of the alternative methods which are presented for stakeholder consideration, criteria and standards for interpreting results, and the potential usefulness of anticipated results. A better design probably results from such thinking and another big plus is that the agreed upon design becomes a contract which protects the client-stakeholder(s) and the evaluator.

The selection of alternative one--decide to evaluate--would seem to assume that the question of being evaluable had been answered in the affirmative. An example of that not being the case would be if the purchaser wanted evidence to cancel a program; an EA would have identified vulnerable aspects of a program and made that effort quicker and less costly!

2. DECIDE TO CHANGE THE PROGRAM

Regardless of the purpose of the EA, this course of action will probably be selected more often than the others for it is hard to imagine studying a program (or plan) with the thoroughness of an EA and not discovering ways it could be improved. (And, as indicated earlier, experience has shown this to be the case.) This alternative would be warranted, for example, if stakeholders were found to have expectations about a program's intents and/or activities that were different from those of the program staff--and the staff considered their expectations valid. It would be warranted if parts of the program were found to be implausible--in which case activities would be added, dropped, or changed.

One way of proceeding would be to identify a group (task force, panel of experts, etc.) to take on the questionable program element(s) as a project to think of ways to correct its reasons for being considered implausible. This assignment could mean coming up with something new, e.g., here is an objective, figure out a way to make it happen; or searching other programs for successful strategies.

When the problem is lack of agreement about what constitutes evidence of performance or when no operational definition of performance can be defined, e.g., what is an innovative program, the recommendation may be to declare that something will meet expectations if certain individuals say it does, e.g., in CES a program could be declared innovative if a panel of peer agents, and the state specialists say it is; in a school district, if a panel of teachers declare it so; etc.

The latter recommendation should be used very sparingly and only for objectives which are of great importance to the organization but elusive in terms of criteria for demonstrating achievement. The procedure should not be used as a substitute for diligently searching for concrete criteria, i.e., as a substitute for laziness.

3. DECIDE TO TAKE NO FURTHER PROGRAM ACTION

If the purpose of the EA was program improvement, no further program action may be needed by the time an EA has reached this stage. Some of what the EA was initiated to do may have already been accomplished. For example, evidence would already be available for stakeholders concerned about the clarity of definition of a program. And, as happened in the CES studies and in those reported by Jung and Schubert (1983), the staff may already have taken steps to correct identified weaknesses in their programs.

If the purpose was to plan a program, the tests of plausibility may have been met and thus no changes considered necessary in the plan. The followup action would be to proceed with implementation.

It is hard to imagine this alternative resulting from an EA conducted with the intent of following up with an intensive evaluation. If the first or second alternatives were not selected as followup (evaluate or change the program), then why initially have invested in the EA?

4. DECIDE TO STOP THE PROGRAM

This alternative could be selected regardless of the purpose of the EA. If the program (or plan) has been found implausible and no solutions can be identified to rectify it, or none that are feasible, or none that stakeholders are willing to invest in, then the best course of action for the organization may be to stop putting resources into it. It could also be warranted if no stakeholders (beyond those who commissioned the EA) are found who think a program is important.

When this course of action is taken, the EA has served a summative evaluation function. That is not an intent of an EA but it certainly could be an outcome. However, if a program is considered worthy of spending resources on to conduct an EA, it probably is worth continuing with at least the next step in Wholey's (1979) suggested sequential purchase of information, before the "cancel program" decision is made.

5. DO NOT DECIDE; IGNORE THE EA

This course of inaction could be taken (1) if the EA was done under the auspices of those who have no power to affect major program decisions (in which case it probably should not have been conducted) or (2) if the EA took so long to complete that decision makers lost interest and/or the program changed significantly from the time data were collected and reported or (3) if there was a change in program leadership during the course of the EA.

The advice here for dealing with the first two possibilities is to take action up front to prevent their occurrence, e.g., make sure there is a defined user and use for data before implementing the study and carry out the EA in as speedy a fashion as possible. And, if the third possibility occurs, meet with the new program leader to describe the EA process and the rationale for the study, and to learn his/her decision needs. The results in their present form may be as useful to the new leader as the one previous or they may can be put in such a form and/or some additional data collected. The point here is that if important information about the program emerged from the EA, it should be relevant in some form to the new leader and effort should be made to make it palatable to him/her.

CHAPTER THIRTEEN

Observations about
the Process

Evaluability assessments were conducted in five states with six different major program areas of the Cooperative Extension Service as a means to define the process in a practical methodological sense and to encourage its adoption in that organization. Implementation proceeded iteratively, one after the other, 1984 to 1989. After each iteration, procedures were analyzed and revised to clarify, and where possible, to simplify to make the process more usable and more "operator robust." EAs were conducted with the intent of improving a later impact study, with the intent of improving an existing program, and finally, the process was used to plan a plausible, evaluable program. We learned much about the process during these field trials, as well as about our programs.

In Chapter Two, many benefits of EA were described that accrue to the organization, to the program under scrutiny, and to the staff involved in the EA. The purpose of this chapter is to reflect on the process itself, based on experiences with the CES studies. Some of the observations focus on the underlying philosophy of the process and others, on methodological considerations.

EA IS BASED ON AN UNDERLYING ASSUMPTION OF RATIONALITY, AND THE WORLD IS NOT SO RATIONAL

Evaluability assessment is based on an assumption that organizations and their programming efforts are tightly coupled and highly structured or will be at the conclusion of the EA (Holloway, 1981). It is based on a rational model of organizational decision making with corresponding assumptions of evaluability very close to that of the problem solving model, i.e.:

o   clearly defined and measurable goals agreed to by managers and policy makers at higher levels
o   plausible activities (means) designed to achieve the goals (ends)
o   causal hypotheses linking means and ends (a discernible logic).

Further assumptions of rationality are that THE decision-makers can be identified and that programs will remain static long enough for some model of program behavior to be appropriate and measurable. In other words, programming is depicted as a deliberate process: first we think, then we act; first we formulate, then we implement.

As much as some of us--especially us evaluators--would like to see this orderly process in programs, in many practical situations the assumptions underlying the rational model do not hold. The result is that many programs are unable to meet the criteria for evaluability--none of the CES programs studied could when the EAs began, at least not explicitly, nor did most of the 57 HHS and Education programs whose EA results were analyzed by Rog (1985).

I am well aware that EA was conceived, at least to a great extent, as an evaluator's coping mechanism for this lack of rationality in programs. Instead of developing his/her own program design and evaluating it--as had been done with little success, in terms of evaluations influencing programming decisions--the evaluator would try to identify those areas of design "fog" which would disable an evaluation. Only when these were resolved would the usual measurement steps commence.

The problem, though, is what do you do when the "unevaluable" conclusion is reached? If you are an "outside" consultant, as we operated in four of the six CES EAs, you can make the "unevaluable" observation and leave the program staff and stakeholders to decide whether and what changes to make OR you can stick around and change from doing evaluability assessment to evaluability creation--which is what we did. No procedures were developed by the EA conceptualizers for this departure from "evaluability" assessment. We learned by trial and error. Those lessons evolved into defining EA as having three equally important purposes--evaluation improvement, program improvement, and program development (planning). This book describes the strategies which worked for us.

I am no longer too bothered that a program may start off with no plausible theory of goal attainment, if in hindsight, plausibility can be discerned, if program staff are able to make explicit what had been implicit plausibility and/or to change program plans to build in the plausibility.

THE EA PROCESS EMPHASIZES MEANS RATHER THAN ENDS

The successful organization is one which gets the right things done (Drucker, 1966). This requires doing the right things and doing them effectively. EA focuses on the second part of the success formula--doing things effectively--as does most other types of evaluation. EA was intended to help assure that program designs would stand a reasonable chance of accomplishing the agreed-upon purposes, prior to evaluation --it was not intended to question those purposes.

In top-down designed programs--which is the kind that EA was originally designed for and the kind it has primarily been used for (Rog, 1985)--not questioning program goals may be a rational decision, because the public pays the Congress, the Executive Branch, and other high level officials to debate and decide upon the purposes of legislated programs. However, in programs designed more from the bottom up, as

CES programs are, questioning end goals or at least questioning the congruence between these goals and evidence of need, seems a logical part of defining assumptions, especially if it is the program staff, who are often the program developers, doing or at least involved in the questioning, and especially if resources are scarce.

A point here is that IF evaluation is to be useful in the social problem solving process, all steps in the problem solving approach need to be examined. Three steps in that approach that occur prior to where EA begins are:

1. identification of an important social problem
2. clear definition of the social problem
3. search for and testing of alternative solutions.

These three steps provide the basis for determining the first part of Drucker's success formula--doing the right thing. If these are weak, the ensuing effective implementation of the program is at best a purposeless exercise and at worst, a waste of valuable resources.

I am not so presumptuous as to have a solution (if one is called for), even though we did grapple with this issue in the CES studies. For example, the California master gardener program's ultimate goal was changed as a result of raising this merit question. The program was first defined in terms of releasing the agent from certain activities. It was finally defined in terms of enabling citizens to solve their horticulture-related problems.

Shadish (1987) said someone must have the courage to say that a program has no merit, if that, in fact, is believed to be the case. Merit may lie in the appropriateness of the goals for the problem at hand and/or it may lie in the appropriateness of the means to reach the goals. It seems to me that both are fair game for an evaluability assessment whose purpose is program improvement.

THE DEVELOPMENT OF MULTIPLE MODELS OF AN ONGOING PROGRAM IS HARD TO DO AND HARDER STILL TO JUSTIFY DOING

Wholey (1979) described the development of four different models, and sometimes more than one of each, as tasks in the process of completing an EA; Nay and Kay (1982) described the use of three models; and Rog's (1985) analysis of 57 EAs found three models to be common. At the beginning of the CES studies, attempts were made to develop three models but the process simply did not work: knowledge was insufficient among program managers and other high-level stakeholders to develop a definitional model, as described by Wholey (1979); program staff found it confusing to deal with several models; and sometimes too much effort seemed to be going to displaying information rather than to specifying the content for the theory. This issue was resolved by developing one model of the program--one as close to implementation reality as possible.

THERE ARE MANY PERCEPTIONS OF "REALITY" AND PROGRAM IMPLEMENTORS AND EA IMPLEMENTORS OFTEN CONFUSE THEM

Developing and validating the program model requires discussions of "reality" at several points. First, deciding who should be involved in the explication of the theory model raises the question of "whose conception of reality is to be tested." Most programs probably have more than one reality and more than one correct program theory can be developed by using different sets of explanatory variables.

Second, in the development of the model, program staff sometimes vacillate between describing what they are doing and what they suddenly realize they probably ought to be doing. From a program improvement viewpoint, this vacillation does not matter, if the "ought to" changes do get incorporated. However, when both real and ideal modeling are going on simultaneously, there is a danger of the staff not being totally conscious of which is which and perceiving the final product (model) as an indication that the program is okay and then not going ahead and making the "ought to" changes; and/or, using the final model to communicate to stakeholders as a picture of present reality. The point here is that it is important for the staff to become fully cognizant of the discrepancy between reality and rhetoric--between what they are doing and any needed changes. Otherwise, the program goals may not be achieved; stakeholder expectations may be erroneously increased; and the program personnel could wind up in a more precarious position relative to program continuance than before the EA began--because the ideal (and perhaps advertised) model is not the reality.

A procedure for making this discrepancy clear is to begin model development by asking program staff to identify everything they do which they consider to be a part of the program. These activities are grouped into what appears to be key components and supporting activities and the model depicted on large sheets of paper visible to the whole group and accessible for changes by the whole group. The staff then verify or change the model to fit reality as they see it; different colored pens are used to make "corrections." This exercise almost always reveals gaps between what is and what is desirable and the colors make the differences obvious.

The third place "reality" becomes an issue is in validating the model developed by the program work team. It was accepted from the beginning that variations would be evident in the same program as implemented at different sites, since Extension programs are operated under a tradition of local control with discretion based on local needs and demands. However, for the program to have integrity, variation should be found to occur mostly in supporting activities and not so much in the underlying logic.

No substantial variation across sites was found in underlying logic for the master gardener or 4-H programs but sufficient variation was found in the different counties for the water quality/quantity program to raise questions about plausibility and to change the purpose of the EA to one of program development. Thus, we did not have to deal with this third reality/rhetoric dilemma. However, when substantial variation is found to occur, we know that the different parties to the EA should debate what is acceptable in the way of variation and what is not. An evaluation can be designed to measure the disparate programs but it must be decided how much variation is to be tolerated.

EVALUATORS MAY LOSE (THE APPEARANCE OF) PROGRAM OBJECTIVITY IN AN EA

In each of the three purposes for implementing an EA, the conductor becomes very involved in the program. In each case, involvement with the staff is intense and personal, especially as assumptions and values surface, as they must in theory definition. In later steps of the EA, conclusions of evaluability (when the purpose is summative) or recommendations for improvement (when the purpose is formative or summative) or conclusions of plausibility (when the purpose is program planning), all represent assessments of program value--all indicate that the program is worthy of investments of additional resources. Although these are appropriate positions for evaluators to take, problems can occur, as Rog (1985) pointed out, when a subsequent evaluation of the program is conducted by the same person who conducted the EA. The problem can be a loss of credibility of evaluation results among those who are in positions to make decisions about the program. One solution is to have the program evaluated by some other individual or group; another is to make sure the evaluation design and subsequent implementation are methodologically above reproach.

OTHER OBSERVATIONS

A number of other observations are implicit or explicit throughout this text which are significant to the success of the process, e.g.,

o   the importance of high-level administrator involvement.
    Where intense involvement was lacking, studies were
    likely to be incomplete in some way(s) and results
    minimally used.

o   the necessity for careful attention to the selection and
    interviewing   of   non-program-staff   stakeholders.
    Interviewing inappropriate persons and/or asking
    inappropriate questions can result in negative program
    impacts. Only persons who know about the program
    should be contacted and from among this group, only
    those whose decisions can affect a program's future in
    very important ways. And, they should be asked only
    what they are qualified to answer. In most instances, we
    should not be asking them how to deliver a program.

o   the importance of focusing on substance rather than
    form. It is easy to get caught "going through the motions"
    of an EA rather than implementing one at the level
    required for real insight to occur. For example, models
    of programs can be developed that look good on paper
    but lack the depth of content for really explaining
    program theory; stakeholders can be interviewed without
    ever acquiring their true perceptions and concerns about
    the program; observations can be made about
    stakeholder views without any collective understanding
    emerging; etc.

o   the importance of completing all the steps in the EA
    process. The most visible products of an EA are
    finished when the program theory models are completed
    and stakeholder interviews summarized. We found this
    to be a natural "stopping place" for many on the EA
    teams. However, if the hard questions, e.g., about
    plausibility, are not answered, the EA will not be
    complete but more importantly, it will not have resulted
    in one of its most critical outcomes. The EA team
    leader must keep a clear focus of what the process is
    intended to do and motivate the other members of the
    team to continue until that is done.

IN CONCLUSION

The observations made in this chapter have focused on the process rather than the outcomes. It is obvious that we in the CES studies had some questions about that process and altered it where it seemed necessary to increase accomplishment of programmatic and organizational goals. We did not change it sufficiently to change the name of the process--even though many nonevaluator types feel the present name is insufficient for how the process has finally evolved in the CES work.

One of the changes from the original conceptualization of the process, was the intense involvement of the program staff in every step. That change resulted in what I perceive as being one of the most important outcomes of the CES EAs--change in team member attitudes, knowledges, and skills about evaluation and programming. When program staff struggle with theory/model specification, they learn not only about the workings of their programs but also a new way of thinking about program development. deGeus (1988) was right when he said persons working together like this on models actually create a new language among themselves that expresses the knowledge they have all acquired. This creates an enormous amount of energy that translates directly to the organization in two ways: first, staff become committed to the program and the organization--there is a camaraderie and a feeling of "belongingness" that develops among team members as they reveal assumptions and agree on common goals. Second, by coming to understand the patterns they formed or that emerged in their past programming behavior, they become more aware of their capabilities and potential for present and future programming behavior.

As an evaluator, I have always had to learn a great deal about programs, and program staff have learned something about evaluation. But the experience of my own learning, time and time again, did not prepare me for what I feel has been the amount of learning experienced by the work teams about evaluability assessment, about evaluation, and about programming. Each EA has started off the same way with team member reluctance to do the hard work and in all except one, each has ended with the work team imploring others to buy into the results and the process.

A high-level administrator in the California master gardener program EA told an audience at a national meeting of Evaluation Network that after having been in Extension for a lot of years, she had finally learned a practical, workable program development process. The local evaluator on the Illinois government officials program EA said he was a better evaluator as a result of having gone through the experience of the EA. "However, what scares me about the process," he said, "is that it seems to be the answer every way I turn for programming and evaluation."

So, if Cronbach and Associates' 93rd thesis is true, i.e., that "The evaluator is an educator;...success is to be judged by what others learn" (1980, p.11), then evaluability assessment in the Cooperative Extension Service has been successful. Positive outcomes have accrued to staff and to programs.

The Cooperative Extension System

The Cooperative Extension System is the largest informal education organization in the world. It was created in 1914 (Smith-Lever Act) to take knowledge directly to the people of rural America, but has since broadened to include virtually any family regardless of its place of residence. It was based on the belief that human progress could be enhanced if the products of research could be translated to lay language and made available to individuals for higher quality decision making.

The success of this system in developing the world's most productive agriculture has been recognized throughout the world. A report by the Carnegie Corporation stated that the System provides the chief example of a successful adult educational movement in the U. S. and represents, so far, the only success of federal government in providing continuing support in higher education (Sprott, 1977).

This national educational network links research, science, and technology to the needs of people where they live and work. It combines the expertise of federal, state, and local governments:

o The Extension Service at the U.S. Department of Agriculture.
o Extension professionals at each of America's 1862 land-grant universities (in the 50 states, Puerto Rico, the Virgin Islands, Guam, Northern Marianas, American Samoa, Micronesia, and the District of Columbia) and in the Tuskegee University and sixteen 1890 land-grant universities.
o Extension professionals in nearly all of the Nation's 3,150 counties.

Education is the only business of the Extension System--practical education for Americans to use in dealing with the critical issues that impact their daily lives and the Nation's future. The national initiatives recently identified for the focusing of educational efforts include:

o Alternative Agricultural Opportunities
o Building Human Capital
o Competitiveness and Profitability of American Agriculture
o Conservation and Management of Natural Resources
o Family and Economic Well-being
o Improving Nutrition, Diet, and Health
o Revitalizing Rural America
o Water Quality

Professionals in agriculture, natural resources, home economics, human nutrition, rural and community development, and 4-H and youth programs focus their educational efforts on these initiatives.

The team which delivers programs is made up of the land-grant college specialist--who is many times also a researcher and teacher--and county staff located in communities where the people and the day-to-day problems exist. They are joined by thousands of volunteer leaders who assist with program implementation, and by local advisory boards/committees which help identify problems and set priorities.

The character of CES education permits the development of new programs as new needs and problems are identified--which means that identification of current needs/problems is a constant requirement. These problems are made known to research faculty who provide content for the curricula aimed at the problems and, if the content is not known, develop research to answer the questions.

Program plans are largely developed at the county level by Extension faculty and advisory committees and are then implemented by county staff with the assistance of state specialists and volunteers.

People participate in programs on a voluntary basis. And, if the programs fail to satisfy their expectations, they may decide to drop out (though they are encouraged to suggest alternatives they think will meet their needs).

Extension's methods provide technical assistance and advice through the dissemination of information, materials, and the use of individual and group problem-solving techniques. The purpose is to help people help themselves to make personally meaningful and satisfying change.

Evaluability Assessment of the
4-H Youth Program*
Maryland Cooperative Extension Service
M. F. Smith**

EXECUTIVE SUMMARY

The Cooperative Extension Service is continually changing its programs to make them more effective in meeting people's needs and more efficient in use of the public's resources. To this end, an evaluability assessment was initiated on Maryland's 4-H program in November, 1985, and completed in May, 1986.

Evaluability assessment is a process for describing a program, and assessing the plausibility of planned and/or implemented activities bringing about intended effects. Data are secured from key external stakeholders as well as program staff, volunteers, and printed program documents.

In this assessment of the 4-H program in Maryland, 43 persons representing seven groups of stakeholders were interviewed and asked the full range of questions. The seven groups were: (1) business leaders and state officials, (2) leaders of community agencies and groups, (3) University of Maryland administrators, (4) state 4-H faculty, (5) county 4-H faculty, (6) other Extension faculty, and (7) 4-H volunteers. Another 53 persons made input on specific aspects of program functioning. National and state program directional documents were reviewed as well as project materials and an earlier study of 4-H.

Conclusions

1. Four-H was very highly regarded by the majority of persons interviewed.
2. There is a lack of clarity among the interviewee groups about the overall mission of 4-H.
3. There was some lack of agreement between 4-H faculty and the other stakeholders about the audience of 4-H.

---

*Excerpts from full report.
**Associate Professor and Coordinator, Program Planning and Evaluation, Cooperative Extension Service, University of Maryland, College Park.

4. The effects of 4-H were seen by all seven groups of interviewees as primarily social in nature. Mental and physical development skills receive. equal billing in directional documents about 4-H but not so among stakeholders.

5. Activities for most of the events were questionable in terms of meeting intended program effects on youth, volunteers, family of 4-H youth, and on the community. Reasons for questioning plausibility were:
   o   an overall plan for the curriculum was not obvious
   o   procedures and criteria for recruiting volunteers were not defined
   ovolunteer competency requirements have not been defined
   o   training for volunteers is not formalized and is sometimes not done
   o   volunteer training in life skills development appears to not be happening
   o   agents feel unprepared to teach volunteers in the life skills area
   o   specific activities with youth to bring about effects were not identified
   o   management of volunteers appears to lack direction.

6. Resources were seen as adequate by a majority of the stakeholders for the present level of program participation.

7. Stakeholders were interested in receiving evaluative information about 4-H, e.g., who really participates, effectiveness of 4-H in reaching its goals, and data to help define the 4-H county faculty member role.

Probably the most serious and far-reaching question which surfaced in this study was: What is the curriculum? If the curriculum can be anything in which youth are interested or is a product of the skills and interests of those who volunteer--which some interviewees thought was the case, then similar observations might be made about 4-H as was about the undergraduate college curriculum by a national committee in 1985*, that is, is the curriculum an invitation to develop life skills--as the state and national documents imply --or is it a quick exposure to content in a specific project area? Or is it both? Certainty on such matters appears to have disappeared and has invited the intrusion of projects of ephemeral knowledge some of which were developed and presented without concern for the criteria of self discovery, leadership ability, communication skills, and exploration of values that have long been considered as central to the 4-H experience. The curriculum appears to have given away to the Marketplace philosophy: a supermarket where youth are the shoppers and volunteers and Extension staff are the merchants. Fads and fashion, the demands of popularity, enter where wisdom, experience, and a sound research base should prevail.

As noted by that committee*, "the Marketplace philosophy refuses to establish common expectations and norms." And, if these are missing, realistic planning cannot occur. Faculty will not know when they have adequately performed their roles; they will not know what leaders and other resources are needed; and will not be able to adequately prepare leaders very far in advance. As a result, leaders will have constant questions and county faculty must spend an inordinate amount of time "holding their hands," helping them solve

*Integrity in the College Curriculum. 1985. Washington, D. C.: Association of American Colleges.

problems or figure out what to do next. In addition to the time involved, such lack of structure can lead to inefficiency and/or ineffectiveness on the part of county faculty and cause them to be (feel) overworked, insecure, frustrated, and cause a lot of job turnover. Job turnover is high in 4-H and some interviewees felt that agents are overworked and frustrated.

Recommendations

1. Define/Clarify the 4-H mission and communicate it to important stakeholders, especially University administrators and business leaders and elected officials.
2. Change program efforts and/or program objectives to bring about congruence among intended effects, planned activities, and targeted audiences(s).
3. If development of life skills is the intended outcome of the 4-H experience, specify which skills, identify experiences to promote their development, prepare faculty and volunteers to promote the skills in youth, and include life skills content and experiences in each of the projects and other 4-H activities.
4. Define criteria for the minimum 4-H experience in terms of type and number of experiences and/or exposure to subject matter content. Key the criteria to intended effects.
5. Define expectations for youth for the different delivery modes.
6. Establish a basis for recruiting and selecting volunteers.
7. Define the role(s) of volunteers and identify competencies necessary to perform the role(s).
8. Assume a proactive stance in the management of volunteers.
9. Define the job of the 4-H county faculty member and set reasonable expectations for performance.
10. Define, clarify, and make obvious to faculty and other important stakeholders the curriculum of 4-H, i.e., the basis for the program. Questions about mission, about intended effects, about volunteer competence, about faculty role, etc., should all be congruent with one another and that congruence should come from some overriding plan.

PROCEDURE

The evaluability assessment of 4-H answered five overall sets of questions:
1. What are the program goals and objectives? Are they clear? Is there agreement among important stakeholders about what the organization of Extension wants to get from a program as well as what is wanted to happen to an identifiable group of clients in terms of (1) changes in knowledge, attitudes, skills and/or (2) behavioral changes and/or (3) economic or social benefits.

2. What is the curriculum? What activities are planned and/or being implemented? Are they sufficient in terms of type and amount to bring about the attainment of desired effects?
3. What sources are in place or could be called upon to provide evidence of implementation and/or accomplishment?   What are specific indicators that (would) signal program success?
4. What resources are available? Are they sufficient to implement the activities? What are the different stakeholder perceptions of resource adequacy?
5. Who wants to know what about the program? Are the needs and uses for evaluative information defined and realistic?

These questions were answered by interviewing stakeholders* internal and external to the program and by reviewing printed program materials.

When the Maryland study began, the Assistant Director for 4-H named three county faculty members to a task force to assist with identification of stakeholders, definition of the implemented program, and summarization of stakeholder interviews. Also identified were three state 4-H faculty to provide input to the study.

Five groups of potential interviewees were identified: business leaders and state officials, University of Maryland administrators, leaders of community agencies and groups, 4-H volunteers, and non-4-H Extension faculty. Interviews were conducted over a three-month period--November, 1985 - January, 1986.   The Coordinator of CES Program Evaluation interviewed four groups: business leader/state officials, University administrators, county and state faculty. An experienced interviewer was hired to interview the others. Specific questions asked of each group and individuals interviewed are listed in Appendix I.**

While interviews were being conducted, the implemented program was described by two sets of county 4-H faculty. The task force--representing three counties--described activities, resources used to carry out the activities, and indicators/sources of evidence of implementation and/or accomplishment. Concurrently but separately, three faculty from one county described what they do to implement the 4-H program. The description from the task force was then shared with the one-county group and vice versa. The two descriptions were very, very similar. Upon review, both groups agreed to a combined description as a "generic" model of 4-H as it is implemented in the field.

The interviews were summarized by the Coordinator for CES Program Evaluation and validated by the task force. A copy of the summary that they judged as an accurate and objective assessment of interviewee comments is included in Appendix III.**

As the study progressed, questions arose about leader training and life skills development. As a result, 53 other persons were asked for input: (a) three 4-H faculty from three counties were randomly selected for input on leader training; (b) one volunteer (chance meeting) from Garrett County was

---

*A "stakeholder" is a person or group with a stake in the program--those who can influence the program in important ways.
**Appendices referred to in these excerpts are those in the full-length 4-H report; they are not included here.

asked about his specific leader training experiences, and (c) 49 randomly selected club volunteers from four counties (part of another evaluative effort) rated their own leader training and identified training needs.

The written documents reviewed and cited in this study were:

o   A future directions document on 4-H developed by a national panel. The final revision, January 31, 1986, entitled 4-H Future Focus was recognized by the Extension Committee on Policy in February, 1986.

o   The latest (1983) University of Maryland 4-H Department Program Direction document.

o   A sample of project manuals: Four project leader manuals and two member manuals (six different projects).

o   The report of a national study of 4-H: Kenneth E. Pigg and James M. Myers. 1980. Social and Economic Consequences of 4-H; Volume I. Washington, D. C.: USDA.

The summary of stakeholder interviews was used to differentiate stakeholder perceptions on mission and goals, program audience, program effects, resource adequacy, and need for information about the 4-H program. The interview summary, input from the other 53 persons, the program model as described by county faculty, and the program as described in the written documents were used to draw conclusions about the plausibility of the program as described in accomplishing intended effects.

Stakeholder perceptions and plausibility conclusions are included in the next main section of this report.   Recommendations based on this assessment are presented in the final section.

ASSESSMENT OF 4-H PROGRAM

Basis for Conclusions

Overall Perceptions about 4-H

Conclusion: Among the groups interviewed, 4-H has a very positive reputation.

Examples of positive comments include:
o   It's wonderful...the best thing for kids
o   Fantastic program
o   Wonderful organization
o   Does outstanding job with youngsters
o   A good traditional program
o   Has lots to offer kids from all economic levels.

The only negative comments came from leaders of community agencies and groups and from other Extension faculty:
o   Not sure it reaches into minority community as much as it should

o   Has less focus on project development, completion and presentation (than it should)
o   Not much creativity in Maryland 4-H for an awfully long time
o   4-H has not used skills available to them.

Overall Question I: Mission, Goals, Effects

A. Are mission and goals clear?

Conclusion: There is a lack of clarity about the overall mission of 4-H and some lack of agreement among the stakeholders and between persons directly involved in implementing the program and those not.

Thirty-five percent of the non-4-H staff interviewees did not know the mission of 4-H, did not articulate one, or else felt the goal was to get more people into the program. As a group, more University administrators were unsure or felt that 4-H was unsure about its mission and more volunteers felt they knew what 4-H was trying to accomplish.

Three business leaders or state officials and one university administrator mentioned agriculture in some way as a part of the mission of 4-H, e.g., "introduce youth to farm life," "sense of responsibility in agriculture and home economics area," "better understanding of production of food," and "better understanding of total food and agricultural system." None of the others, including the 4-H State staff, mentioned agriculture as a part of the mission.

Technology transfer, which historically was a mission of 4-H, was mentioned as a mission by only one person and that was a member of the 4-H State staff. One university administrator noted technology transfer as a historical mission but asked "Is 4-H doing what it should in 1985?"

The most agreement about the mission of 4-H was by 4-H staff and active volunteers who saw it as developing life skills or other skills. The most agreement by those not actively involved in 4-H saw it as getting more people involved.

County faculty identified specific effects they thought the program has on youth and volunteers (see next section) but felt the state mission was to increase the number of enrolled youth. They felt these intended effects were important but that all their emphasis had to be put on recruitment because the bottom line at performance appraisal time is "how many youth are enrolled?"

B. Is it clear who is to be effected--who is the audience.?

Conclusion: There is some lack of agreement between 4-H faculty and the other stakeholders about the audience of 4-H.

Nearly half (45%) of the nonfaculty stakeholders disagreed with the 4-H staff about who is the audience for 4-H. Others wondered if the actual audience of 4-H were those who needed it most.

Written documents on 4-H, and state and county 4-H faculty members identified the audience of 4-H as youth and adults:

o   Any youth aged 8-18 has been the traditional audience of 4-H but recently six and seven-year-olds have been targeted.

o   Adult volunteers who assist with program implementation.

Variants to the faculty position were:

o   Two state officials and one agency representative identified the audience as only rural, farm-related youth.

o   One university administrator and one other Extension faculty member said it was for middle-class youth.

o   One agency representative said adults were definitely not an intended audience.

o   Two volunteers limited the youth audience to those who are achievers and those who have interests in the 4-H project areas.

o   One volunteer said 4-H was definitely not for all youth and that 4-H should not "take a lot of time away from satisfying those who are in it ... to try to inspire minorities" or others to join.

o   Only one person (community agency representative) thought eight-year-odds were intended recipients and no one, other than 4-H faculty, singled out younger kids.

o   Two persons (state official and university administrator) wondered if the youth 4-H actually worked with were those who needed 4-H the most or if they would have achieved anyway. In other words, do they become leaders because of 4-H or were they leader-types anyway?

C. Is there agreement about intended effects?

Conclusion: Social, mental, and physical development were listed as the program objectives in the state program direction document. There was agreement among all group and in written documents that the effects of 4-H are primarily social in nature, e.g., self confidence/self esteem, leadership, citizenship. There was less agreement about its effects on mental development and no agreement between written objectives and interviewees about its impact on physical development.

Since only one non-4-H faculty member identified adults as an audience of 4-H, this question on clarity and agreement about effects will focus only on those intended for youth.

The Maryland 4-H Program Direction document and the National 4-H Future Focus agree for the most part that intended effects of 4-H are in the areas of social and mental development. The state document adds a third area not mentioned in the national document: physical development (health and safety). None of the interview groups mentioned any effects in physical development. The greatest agreement across the different interview groups, faculty, and written documents was in four subtopics of the social development skills: leadership, communication, self confidence/self esteem, and community awareness/involvement. A fifth area, personal standards and values was listed by only two groups--state faculty and community agency representatives.

The six mental development skills (management, education, and knowledge transfer) were essentially overlooked except for career awareness (recognized by county faculty, volunteers, and state officials) and decision making (recognized by state faculty, a university administrator, and a community representative). Using time wisely, developing a conservation attitude, and developing an inquiring mind were not mentioned by any group including state and county faculty. Only faculty mentioned the fourth subarea under mental development--learning practical knowledge in project areas. No one talked about sharing or transferring that knowledge.

Thirty-nine percent of the non-4-H faculty interviewees did not state any specific effects that 4-H had on its audience. The further removed the group was from the everyday 4-H activities, the fewer of them who were knowledgeable about effects, e.g., all the volunteers but only a third of the business leader/state officials group identified effects. A difference occurred in areas of interests: volunteers felt that if a youth already had an interest, he/she could develop it in 4-H; state faculty felt that the 4-H experience allowed youth to identify new interests.

The county faculty, as a group, credited 4-H with more knowledge/skills acquisition than did the state faculty or other groups. Volunteers placed especially heavy emphasis on self confidence and the positive effects of youth interaction with non-school and non-family-member adults.

Faculty employed in 4-H identified _far_ _fewer_ effects of 4-H than did the volunteers or the other interviewees who were further removed from the program. The volunteers and other interviewees were also much more specific in their descriptions of the effects than were the state and county faculty.

Overall Questions II and III and Part of IV: Curriculum Plausibility

A. What activities are implemented?

Six agents from four counties described "what they do" to implement the 4-H program. Three agents from three counties worked as one group to define activities, indicators/sources of performance, and approximate resources used to carry out the activities. Three other agents from one county worked as a group to define activities. Both groups later reacted to each other's definitions and agreements were made on a "generic" model of the 4-H program.

The logic and flow of the program was laid out as a series of If-Then statements to form a hypothesis trail in a causal sequence, i.e., if staff do certain things then other things will happen to clients and/or to whoever/whatever the program impacts. The hypothesis trail is _not_ laid out on a strict time sequence, e.g., recruiting and training volunteers goes on all year though the greatest emphasis is in late summer and fall. (See Addendum One for the program logic model--Figure II-1--and a description of activities implemented to achieve the separate components.)

B. Are individual events plausible?

Two questions are answered to determine plausibility--Are events/activities well defined? and, Are they sufficient in type and amount?

Event 1. Agents and Volunteers Recruit and Select Volunteers

    1.a. **Purpose is identified and clear.**
    1.b. **Activities are identified; plausibility is questionable.**
    1.c. **Resources are not clearly identified so the plausibility question is not applicable.**
    1.d. **Performance indicators/source are identified and appear plausible for the activities listed if criteria and standards are identified for successful performance.**

The basis for recruiting and selecting volunteers is not apparent. A very good county faculty member who is experienced, conscientious, and "on-top" of the total county program may be able to informally and intuitively determine the number and types of volunteers needed. One less experienced and/or less conscientious may not know how or take the time to go about the process in an effective way.

Without a defined procedure and/or a set of criteria, agents are left to take whatever shows up in the form of volunteers. This could lead to "accepting" more volunteers than can be used in some areas--rather than having a basis for asking if they could participate at a later time--and not being able to selectively recruit to have enough in others. The former situation can result in persons being turned off because they were never utilized in the program; the latter can result in assigning volunteers outside their areas of expertise and/or the county faculty member having to implement a lot of what should be volunteer activities.

Event 2. Agents and Volunteers Train Volunteers

    2.a. **Purpose is identified and clear.**
    2.b. **Activities are identified; the plausibility of this training leading to desired effects is questionable.**
    2.c. **Resources are clearly identified and appear plausible for the activities listed.**

2.d. **Performance indicators/sources were identified and appear plausible for the activities listed, if criteria and standards are identified for successful performance.**

If all described activities were implemented on a consistent basis with all volunteers, the event should achieve its purpose of orienting volunteers to 4-H and CES and prepare them to assist youth in acquiring many of the knowledge effects listed in Event 6. The training would most likely not prepare them to help youth achieve the skills known as life skills.

According to the county faculty, the activities identified for training volunteers represent the ideal. They indicate that no one county is probably implementing all the activities and some may be doing very few. Each of the agents making input was doing some of them. Part of the reason for this discrepancy is that the number and types of volunteers differ from county to county as does the extent and formalness of the training. There is no specified curriculum for training volunteers; and county and state faculty and the volunteers themselves say they are not getting the training and guidance they need. County faculty also say many volunteers will not participate when training is offered.

Early in the conduct of this evaluability assessment, the question arose as to leader training being adequate in amount and type to lead to youth developing the intended life skills. Since leaders play such an important role in the implementation of the program, additional data were secured, beyond the usual evaluability assessment, to enable better-supported conclusions on this question:

1. In addition to the six county faculty defining the 4-H Model (Addendum One), three agents from three counties were selected at random and asked to describe what they do in the way of leader training with specific emphasis on how they prepare volunteers to teach life skills.
2. A random sample of club volunteers in four counties (Anne Arundel, Frederick, Howard, and Prince George's) were surveyed by telephone in April, 1986, and asked to rate their leader training and to identify what they felt they needed that their training did not provide.
3. A chance meeting with a volunteer from Garrett County permitted specific questions on his training.
4. Six project manuals (four leader and two youth) were analyzed for leader guidance in life skills development.

4-H Faculty Assessment of Leader Training

One agent of nine (11%) indicated his county provided formal training for each volunteer and annual updates. Some of the others hold one-on-one sessions as needed or "group meetings several times a year" and invite all leaders to participate. One agent pointed out, though, that very few leaders generally show up for these sessions. Another said a big problem they had was convincing leaders they needed training. That is understandable if there are no specific competencies identified that a leader must have and/or no specific body of knowledge that they should know.

Most agents indicated that at least one session was held with a new organizational (club) leader to plan the first six months' plan for the club. At this time the person would generally be given a book or some handouts explaining about CES, affirmative action guidelines, etc. After that, the person would be invited to group sessions held every four to six months.

None of the nine agents indicated that his/her leader training identified or defined the specific effects (life skills) that youth are supposed to develop/refine. Responses indicative of all nine follow to the question "When and how do you teach volunteers how to teach life skills?"

o   We don't.
o   One we push very strongly in this county is public speaking. Every other year we have a session to train leaders on public speaking, e.g., how to motivate the kids to want to talk, how to actually give a talk, steps to making a speech, and so forth.
o   We don't do much on that; we rely mostly on written materials and we hope that they read these.
o   Each of the programs we work with, any activity, has built in some form of life skills. You can't take it without getting experience in some of these.
o   Leaders would get bogged down if we told them all about life skills. Some of the leaders may not have more than a seventh grade education themselves. They may know a lot about food buying, for example, but not be academically oriented to things like the process areas. Also they may not know the decision making process themselves.

County faculty felt they needed more assistance in this area. One director of a county/city unit said "My agents do not know how to train volunteers." An agent said "We could use more training in this area; could use more expert advice on how to teach these life skills."

Another question asked was "Will volunteers know they are teaching these skills when they are implementing activities?" Representative responses were:
o   Leaders might not know they're teaching decision making (for example) but we know it, if they teach the projects.
o   Leaders may not know they are teaching the life skills but they are doing some of the things that are important for kids to do.

Responses by the state 4-H faculty to these same questions were as follows:
o   I doubt that we're training our volunteers enough, period...I think most volunteers will know they're teaching life skills. However, there is a gap between having this and having people working with youth exercising or practicing it. If they knew better then there might not be a need for so many materials written for youth.

o   Most faculty and volunteers don't have the background to deal in these process areas. That is what distinguishes an excellent agent from a good agent.

o   Agents in Maryland are good teachers, but they may not have to be a good teacher to be good at process skills.

o   Life skills are taught indirectly by adapting the subject matter to the purpose. ...we see livestock judging as developing decision making skills though the person involved probably just sees that he or she is judging livestock. We don't attract kids into the program by saying they will learn life skills, we do it on the basis of things they will learn and the recognition they will receive. Kids are more aware afterwards that they were learning decision making, they may not know at the time.

o   The life skills are probably not taught enough in the subject matter...volunteers are not receiving the training they need.

Volunteer Assessment of Leader Training

The twelve volunteers who were interviewed specifically for the evaluability assessment were <u>not</u> asked questions about their training. However, three mentioned training when they were asked if they had any concerns about how the program is implemented. One said "4-H loses leaders because they just get overwhelmed and discouraged." Another said she had never been told what she was expected to do and that she needed help.

The volunteer from Garrett County said he did <u>not</u> receive training or suggestions from CES on how to teach life skills. He felt that was okay, in fact, "it is better as a leader if you learn as you go. I just praise the kids and they do good on their own."

In April, 1986, forty-nine club volunteers randomly selected from Anne Arundel, Frederick, Howard, and Prince George's counties were contacted by telephone, in a study separate from this evaluability assessment. One part of the survey pertained to volunteer appraisal of leader training. They were asked, "How would you rate the leader training you received on a scale of 1 to 5, with 1 meaning "great preparation for my club work" to 5 meaning "poor preparation for my club work." Sixty-seven percent (33) gave a negative rating to their training (3, 4, or 5).* Among these, 36% (12) said they received no training or made other comments which implied no training, e.g., learned on own or asked other leaders for help.

To the question, "What do you feel you needed in the way of training that you did not get?" thirty percent (10) mentioned general leader training, e.g., role of leader, how to be effective leader, leader workshops; 24% felt the need for training on how to operate a club, e.g., how 4-H club operates, how to start a new club, how to recruit members; 18% wanted more contact with the 4-H professional. Other training needs mentioned were: leader

---

*A 3, which <u>might</u> be considered as neutral, was rated as a negative response because further comments by these raters showed their appraisals to be as negative as those rating training the worst--a 5.

handbooks, more leader-to-leader discussions, paperwork requirements, how to work with parents, how to keep youth interested, how to do record books, and information on what 4-H is and its goals. One leader noted that "there is a lack of promotion for training sessions on the county level...it's hard to train leaders if they do not come to the workshops."

Only one of this group made a comment about training that could be construed as positive: "maintain it as it is." Fifty percent (8) of those who rated their training above average or great (a 4 or a 5) made positive comments, e.g., constantly being trained, they do a good job, materials are excellent, good cooperation. Twenty-five percent (4) suggested training or assistance deficiencies, e.g., training on record books is poor, should have taken more time on how to put a club together, should be a package of materials for leaders sent to them all at once--not in pieces, need more county agent visits.

Life Skills development guidance in project manuals.

One of the consistent comments by faculty about leader training was that if leaders and youth do what is suggested in their project booklets, youth will learn the life skills. To determine the probability of this occurring the evaluator went to the state 4-H office and asked the secretary for four to six project leader manuals. No specific ones were requested. The secretary selected four manuals for leaders: Learn and Earn, Horse Project Lesson Outline, Dairy Project, and Dog Care and Training, and two for youth: You and Your Money, and Advanced Clothing.

These manuals were evaluated on two criteria: (1) were life skills defined in the objectives and (2) were suggestions included on specific ways leaders might assist life skills development. Only one of the four leader manuals (Learn and Earn) met both criteria. It stated that the leader is to provide "learning experiences for 4-H youth to develop life skills," specified what those skills were, and provided suggestions for encouraging their development.

The Dog Care and Training manual indicated that training a dog teaches such skills as responsibility, pride in ownership, to make decisions, etc. The manual did not define these in words or by example nor did it suggest how the leader was to work with youth to encourage that development. With the exception of the introduction, the whole manual was on how to have a well-trained and cared-for dog rather than how to have a youngster with increased life skills.

The Dairy Project leader manual made mention only of what youth were expected to learn about dairying and dairy projects plus the objective to "have fun together." The Horse Project outline for leaders provided no background information, no overall goals, and mentioned no life skills--it was a series of lesson plans with stated objectives of teaching some knowledge and/or skill in understanding horses and horsemanship.

You and Your Money member manual never directly stated anything about life skills but it did provide experiences that if repeated would lead to skills development in such things as record keeping, prioritizing expenditures, planning a budget, and money management.

All the objectives in the <u>Advanced Clothing</u> member manual were specifically related to advanced tailoring techniques. The only potential life skill mentioned was the development of appreciation and awareness of the costs involved in ready-to-wear versus custom-tailored garments.

Based on this review of randomly selected (representativeness unknown) project manuals, the chances of youngsters developing the life skills as a result of project participation is a "hit-or-miss" proposition.

A second concern by some about projects, is that completion is not necessarily promoted. Faculty in some counties do not have a defined procedure for determing how many projects are completed. They know how many sign up for them but not necessarily how many complete them. Some volunteers also questioned the need for all youth to complete their booklets. One suggested that only kids who want to become leaders should have to "write stuff."

Event 3. Agents and Volunteers Implement Program

3.a. **Purpose is identified and clear.**
3.b. **Activities are identified but plausibility of them achieving intended effects is questionable.**
3.c. **Resources are not clearly identified, so the plausibility question is not applicable.**
3.d. **Performance indicators/sources were identified and appear plausible for the activities listed, if criteria and standards are identified for successful performance.**

It is not clear what is done with youth to accomplish the intended effects, i.e., What is done with youth to assure they acquire knowledge and skills in the targeted areas? What is done to help them learn about the community and change it? etc. Are these and the other effects accomplished by recruitment and county-wide and special interest workshops? How do youth participate?

Event 4. Agents manage volunteers.

4.a. **Purpose is identified but stated so broad that (1) almost any activity would qualify as relevant and (2) it precludes conclusions about adequacy of activities.**
4.b. **Activities are identified but somewhat vague. Plausibility cannot be determined.**
4.c. **Resources are identified and appear adequate for the activities listed.**
4.d. **Performance indicators/sources are identified and appear plausible for activities listed, if criteria and standards are identified for successful performance.**

(1) The activities appear reactive whereas management as a process suggests a proactive stance is taken to accomplish some given objective(s). This observation is supported somewhat by observations made by interviewees, e.g., one University administrator said "we have lost leadership role as to what 4-H should be. Others are providing leadership rather than us, e.g., volunteers." A volunteer said "we have a great deficit as far as leadership in 4-H."

(2) Management as a function includes four types of activities other than staffing: planning, organizing, directing, and controlling. All four types may be present in this or other events but they are not obvious. For example: Planning to some extent is occurring in Event 2 where volunteer training takes place, especially where new organizational leaders are assisted with their first few club meetings. However, a state 4-H faculty member said one of the greatest weaknesses of the 4-H program is the lack of planning at the local club level. And, some volunteers say they don't know what they are supposed to do.

Planning and organizing is evident in this Event in the scheduling of events and activities and in Event 2 where training is conducted. Organizing is evident in the coordinator roles faculty perform with special interest, school enrichment, and EFNEP activities. Communication seems to be occurring from agent to volunteer but some volunteers say it is not occurring among volunteers and between the state office and the volunteers.

Directing is not obvious. As noted above, the activities appear reactive. Where are the activities which show faculty providing the leadership, as one University administrator noted, "to make sure that whatever we want to happen, does"? Motivation--considered a part of directing--is obvious in the newsletter, phone calls, and annual recognition programs.

Controlling at one level is occurring in activity #9 with record keeping efforts. The aspect of control which is not evident is the establishment of standards and subsequent activities to determine their attainment. This potential weakness was described earlier in terms of lack of specific expectations for volunteer competency.

Event 5. Agents implement other program responsibilities.

5.a **The purpose is identified but is too broad for a clear assessment of plausibility of activities.**

5.b. **Activities are identified.**

5.c. **Resources are identified. However, one might question 30% of each agent's time devoted to mostly nonprogrammatic concerns.**

5.d. **Performance indicators/sources are identified and appear plausible for activities listed, if criteria and standards are identified for successful performance.**

With the exception of #4--Develop Plan of Work--and #10 and #11, they are organizational rather than programmatic. From a programmatic sense, placement of POW development in this event appears out of place in the causal sequence in which this model of the program is laid out. It is not out of place if the POW is done to meet organizational responsibility rather than as a guide for implementation. It is also not out of place if the emphasis in 4-H is to "get more numbers." Some interviewees felt the latter was the case and county faculty say the bottom line at performance appraisal time is how many youth and how many volunteers are enrolled. That supports the logic model showing recruitment as the first step in program development/ implementation and the placement of plan of work development in Event 5.

Plausibility of Events/Activities Achieving Intended Program Effects

The first five events in the program logic model have been examined primarily in terms of individual contributions and purposes. This section will discuss the plausibility of all five in achieving overall program effects--the final four segments in the logic model.

Even if all the activities in Events 1 through 5 were implemented according to plan, there still seems to be a missing link in the Logic Model (Figure 1) in terms of apparent plausibility to bring about the intended effects of the program. The missing link is an event titled something like "Define the Program or "Determine the Curriculum" which should occur before all other events listed.

Development of the plan of work (POW) is presented as a part of Event 5 rather than as a necessary requisite to recruiting and training volunteers and implementing the prevents plausible activities in the first three events, i.e., without a curriculum plan, how can county faculty know what types of leaders they need to recruit? How can they know what to train volunteers to do? How can they and the volunteers know what to implement?

Interviewee observations and concerns support the missing link thesis. The more subtle evidence is that a large number of them did not know the mission of 4-H and questioned if 4-H did. However, one could be unclear on a mission and still have a curriculum or a planned course of study around which definite decisions could be made about what to do. The more direct evidence is comments interviewees made when asked if they had any observations or suggestions about program implementation. They asked questions like "What is the program?" "What is the 4-H experience?" and commented:

o   I am concerned that maybe we don't have a curriculum--that what is taught is more a product of the skills and interest of those who volunteer.
o   Need to identify what we are doing.
o   Need a curriculum that all in 4-H learn.
o   They are trying to shotgun everything.
o   4-H activities are limited by the imagination and resource contacts...(of) volunteer leaders.
o   Emphasis should be on...completion of a course.

If the curriculum can be anything in which youth are interested or is a product of the skills and interests of those who volunteer, then similar observations might be made about 4-H as was about the undergraduate college curriculum by a national committee* in 1985; that is:

Is the curriculum an invitation to develop life skills--as the state and national documents imply--or is it a quick exposure to content in a specific project area? Or is it both? Certainty on such matters appears to have disappeared and has invited the intrusion of projects of ephemeral knowledge some of which were developed and presented without concern for the criteria of self discovery, leadership ability, communication skills, and exploration of values that have long been considered as central to the 4-H experience. The curriculum appears to have given away to the Marketplace philosophy: a supermarket where youth are the shoppers and volunteers and Extension staff are the merchants. Fads and fashion, the demands of popularity, enter where wisdom, experience, and a sound research base should prevail.

As noted by that committee*, "the Marketplace philosophy refuses to establish common expectations and norms." And, if these are missing, realistic planning cannot occur. Faculty will not know when they have adequately performed their roles; they will not know what leaders and other resources are needed; and will not be able to adequately prepare leaders very far in advance. As a result, leaders will have constant questions and county faculty must spend an inordinate amount of time "holding their hands," helping them solve problems or figure out what to do next. In addition to the time involved, such lack of structure can lead to inefficiency and/or ineffectiveness on the part of the county faculty and cause them to be (feel) overworked, insecure, frustrated, and cause a lot of job turnover. Job turnover is high in 4-H and some interviewees felt that agents are overworked and frustrated.

Effects side of Program Model

Effects Occur on Youth

Only one of the effects identified in the program description of 4-H was linked to a particular experience--#7 indicates that only exchange club members acquire knowledge of other peoples and cultures. Are the other six sets of effects expected from participants in clubs as well as those in special interest, school enrichment, and other activities? That assumption would seem invalid based on a preliminary study** which showed considerable variation in the power of the different participation units to bring about change. One of the state 4-H faculty indicated agreement with this difference in potential effect: "...the traits we have to develop will come about in an extended time rather than on a short exposure--time is needed for leadership to develop. Special interest may develop an increase in knowledge but not have the same opportunity for the kid developing personally. That is why we stress club work--for a time for longer term life skills to develop."

*Integrity in the College Curriculum. 1985. Washington, D.C.: Association of American Colleges.
**Kenneth E. Pigg and James M. Myers. 1980. Social and Economic Consequences of 4-H, Volume I. Washington, D. C.: USDA.

In the absence of a standard for the 4-H experience and a definition of basic competency requirements for a volunteer, one cannot adequately evaluate the activities in terms of their potential for bringing about growth or change in enrolled youth. The effects may be occurring with some youth but some interviewees thought that was a consequence of the particular leaders recruited rather than of the 4-H curriculum.

The training for volunteers appears to have the potential to affect knowledge acquisition more so than life skills development and more in the almost any level project areas could lead to increased employability skills (Effect #5) and or participation could lead to Effect #6--Gain experience with adults other than parents and teachers.

Oftentimes, the effects of 4-H are discussed in terms of future impact, e.g., one 4-H state faculty member indicated that youth may not know "at the time" that they are learning or acquiring skills. However, the effects listed by the agents in Maryland focused on the present and the indicators/sources for evaluating the effects were also present based. The latter appear adequate for accountability purposes, if criteria and standards are identified for successful performance.

Effects Occur on Volunteers

The 1983 4-H Department program directions document indicates that the "objective of the...program is to assist youth and adult volunteers in their social, mental, and physical development." However, all the activities listed in Events 1-5 in the program description are designed to impact youth. Specific efforts to impact adults--other than as a tool to reach youth--seem to be missing.

Some leaders may be acquiring some or all of the knowledge and skills listed--those leaders who actually receive formal training. However, it is different to talk with an adult about how to get youth to improve their public speaking skills, for example,and to work with the adult to improve his/her own public speaking skills. And, one might argue that a person does not have to be a good speaker to help another increase skill in that area.

The point here is that the activities listed do not support effects on volunteers as an intended outcome of the program. Some of the effects may occur but they probably are not occurring as frequently as they might if specific effort were made to make them happen.

Among the 43 interviews conducted specifically for this evaluability assessment, only one non-4-H faculty member felt that adults were an audience of the 4-H program.

The indicators/sources appear adequate if criteria and standards are in place, e.g., reviewing copies of records as an indication of improving skills in record keeping would be adequate if criteria were identified for what "good" records are.

Effects Occur on Family of 4-H Members

The same arguments presented for effects on volunteers apply here. No activities are listed to effect members of the family of a 4-H member.

Effects Occur on Community

Effect 1 "Increase in number of volunteers doing community work." This effect occurs every time a new person volunteers and work with 4-H. However, increase in number of volunteers in other community work is not planned for in the activities listed in Events 1-5.

Effect 2 "Community groups get services..." This effect occurs every time 4-H'ers work on community projects--which is probably very often. There are no activities listed, however, which have a purpose of providing services to the community.

Effect 3 "People in community become more aware of minorities..." and Effect 4 "Community is safer..." No activities appear directed toward the community with respect to these effects.

Only the sources listed for effects 2 and 4 appear plausible for hard data to support the effects.

Overall Question IV: Resource Adequacy

Are resources sufficient to implement identified activities of the program? What are stakeholder perceptions of adequacy of resources.

Conclusion: The resources for the 4-H program are probably as adequate as for any other Extension program area, given the present level of participation.

Nearly everyone had an opinion about the adequacy of resources for the 4-H program. Approximately one-third (35%) of all those interviewed felt the resources were inadequate; nearly half (44%) felt they were adequate. The others could not decide (6%) or felt no program was adequately funded now (12%).

The 4-H state staff was the only group unanimous in its rating of resources--inadequate. County faculty did not mention this as an area of great concern when implementation of the program was being described and volunteers were about evenly split in their perceptions. None of the UM administrators, other University faculty, or business leader/state officials groups felt resources were inadequate.

An answer to the question of adequacy of resources can be elusive because it depends if one thinks of adequacy in terms of what is being done or in terms of what someone thinks is needed to be done. For example, the resources might be perceived as adequate for meeting the needs of the number of youth presently in the program but inadequate to reach the number the staff would like to reach. Similarly, the resources may not be adequate to revise all the project manuals, but are all the projects needed? The answer also depends on how resources are being used. If intended effects are not being achieved (a question not addressed in this study), it could be that resources were expended on the wrong activities or that the activities were poorly implemented.

Four-H, like all Extension programs, is more dependent on time of individuals than it is on other resources. Using staff F.T.E. as an index, one might argue that the resources are more than adequate for the number of youth enrolled, as compared to other states. The number reached per FTE in Maryland in 1984-85 was 240 compared to the national average of 375.*

Considering that the overall goal/mission of 4-H and its intended audience are not clearly identified and agreed upon (see Overall Question I), there could be some inefficient and/or ineffective use of resources caused from a lack of focusing of efforts. Stakeholders did in fact mention diversity of curriculum offerings as a concern along with too much effort on increasing numbers.

The 4-H program is implemented primarily through unpaid volunteers. If these volunteers are inadequately trained, they will have difficulty in achieving program objectives plus they will require a lot of paid staff time to answer questions and solve problems. Thus, what is perceived to be inadequate resources (too few paid staff) could in fact be an indication of ineffective volunteer training. The problem would be compounded if faculty were ill prepared for their own roles.

There is some evidence that this could be the case. Leader training tied for first place among interviewees identifying implementation concerns. Eleven persons had some concern about training and several of these were volunteers. One volunteer said he did not know what he was supposed to do; another felt the need for more guidance on how to do what was expected. Several from other interviewee groups wondered if the volunteers were being prepared to teach--especially if they were being prepared to teach life skills.

Agent preparedness was a concern of all six interviewee groups. Some felt they came into the position without needed skills, some felt they received inadequate on-the-job training, and some even questioned if an agent's first job in Extension should be in 4-H, because of the complexity of the job.

If there is no specific curriculum, agents may have difficulty in getting and staying proficient. If the curriculum could be "anything a child is interested in," or is dictated by the interests of the volunteers, both of which some interviewees attest, a county faculty member could feel the need to constantly be learning new subject matter, at least during the first few years in the 4-H position. That can take valuable energy away from implementation activities and cause a great deal of insecurity and frustration--and job turnover. And, as noted previously, job turnover in 4-H is high.

As one interviewee noted, throwing more dollars into the program will not make the problems go away. Identifying the role of the county faculty

---

*F.T.E. = full-time equivalent position. Statistics are from 1984-85 State Annual Reports, Washington, D. C.: ES/USDA.

member and then focusing staff development efforts on that should make a difference, especially if everyone is clear on the program.

Overall Question V: Evaluation Needs

Who wants to know what about the program: Are the needs for evaluative information defined and realistic?

Conclusion: Persons beyond the level of program implementation were clear about the types of data they would like to have on the program and their needs were realistic, e.g., Who does the program serve? What is the program--what is the experience? and What are the results?

Four-H staff were mostly concerned with descriptive information, e.g., What is the 4-H experience? What happens longitudinally from age 9-19? What are youth and volunteer characteristics?   The group of business leader/state officials was mostly interested in who is served by the program, the impact on those served, and if the program was meeting its objectives. University administrators were similarly interested in the audience, especially if it were working with those who might need the program most, and the program's effectiveness but they also wanted information which would be helpful in hiring and keeping faculty--work role, job requirements, and work load.

The areas of agreement about desired data among the three groups were Who does it serve? What is the actual 4-H experience? and What are the results?

Two few individuals responded in the other three groups for group observations to be made. They may, in fact, have had little or no interest in data about the program; however, the way the interviewer phrased the question for most interviewees barely gave them a chance to think about it. One community agency leader did say he would like some "honest figures" on how many completed projects, what was learned, quality of those who don't surface as winners and what happens to them, and turnover rate among agents in 4-H compared to other program areas. One volunteer wanted to know how activities were evaluated, how leaders feel about their leader experience, and how different levels (leaders, members, faculty) perceive the way complaints about events are handled.

For the most part,the needs for evaluative information are consistent with some of the lack of clarity on the program. Some say the mission is not clear so they want to know what the program is intending to do. Some are not clear about the audience so they want to know who it serves.

The intended uses for data were also consistent with what was requested.   State faculty wanted information to help with program implementation decisions, e.g., Which delivery modes are best? What are volunteers like so assignments can be made to better utilize their talents? What are youth interests so they can develop/revise relevant events, activities, and project materials? etc.

University administrators wanted data to justify programs to the legislature and to the citizens of Maryland, e.g., quantifiable evidence of achievement of objectives and specific examples of success stories. They also wanted information to assist with staffing decisions, e.g., definition of what agents do "that can be counted" so a reasonable work load could be determined and appropriate matches could be made between applicants' experiences and training and the expectations of the job.

SUMMARY CONCLUSIONS AND RECOMMENDATIONS

Nearly 100 persons from 14 counties plus Baltimore City provided data about the 4-H program. Conclusions based on this input plus review of program documents are listed below followed by specific recommendations for program improvement.

Conclusions

1. Overall Perceptions: Among the groups interviewed, 4-H has a very positive reputation. Nearly all the 43 interviewees--even those who had no firsthand information on the program--felt that it was a valuable program and youth were better off for having participated.

2. Mission: There is a lack of clarity about the overall mission of 4-H and some lack of agreement among the stakeholders and between persons directly involved in implementing the program and those not. Thirty-nine percent of the non-4-H staff interviewees did not know the mission of 4-H, did not articulate one, or else felt the goal was to get more people into the program. As a group, more University administrators were unsure or felt that 4-H was unsure about its mission.

3. Audience: There is some lack of agreement between 4-H faculty and the other stakeholders about the audience of 4-H. Four-H faculty indicate that any youth are targets of the program and adults who assist with program implementation. Only one of the other stakeholders thought adults were targets of the program. Others thought the program was for a particular type of youth, e.g., rural, middle-class, leader types.

4. Effects: There was agreement among all groups and in the written documents that the effects of 4-H are primarily social in nature, e.g., self confidence/self esteem, leadership, citizenship. There was less agreement about its effects on mental development and no agreement between written objectives and interviewees about its impact on physical development. The six mental development skills (pertaining to management, education, and knowledge transfer) were essentially overlooked except for career awareness and decision making. Faculty was the only group to mention learning practical knowledge in project areas--no one talked about sharing or transferring that knowledge.

5. Program Plausibility: <u>Even if all the activities identified in the definition of the program</u> (See model in Appendix II.) <u>were implemented according to plan, plausibility of these leading to the intended program effects is questionable.</u>   A link appears to be missing from program logic-- something like "Define the Program" or "Determine the Curriculum." This link would appear to be necessary prior to all the other events listed. Lack of such a link prevents plausible activities in the first three events, i.e., without a curriculum plan, how can county faculty know what types of leaders they need to recruit? How can they know what to train volunteers to do? How can they and the volunteers know what to implement?

Plausibility Conclusions by Event:

Event I. Agents and Volunteers Recruit and Select Volunteers. Plausibility of activities achieving the desired outcome is questionable because there is no obvious basis for recruitment and selection; there is no defined procedure and/or set of criteria to guide such effort.

Event II. Agents and Volunteers Train Volunteers. Plausibility of activities appears questionable since there is no formal curriculum for training volunteers; there is no definition of the skills a volunteer must have; training is going on in some counties and not in others; training is going on for some volunteers and not for other.   <u>If</u> all the activities were implemented on a consistent basis with all volunteers, the event should achieve its purpose of orienting volunteers to 4-H and CES, less so in preparing them to assist youth in acquiring many of the knowledge effects, and most likely not prepare them to help youth acquire life skills. County faculty admit they are not providing leaders the training in life skills development and admit that they, themselves do not feel prepared in the life skills area. Sixty-seven percent of the volunteers in a four-county survey gave a negative rating to their training in terms of preparing them for their club work.

Event III. Agents and Volunteers Implement Program. Plausibility of activities appears questionable because it is not clear what is done with youth to accomplish the intended effects. Activities focus on recruitment, affirmative action, solicitation of funds and other resources, problem solving, and countywide and special interest workshops.

Event IV: Agents Manage Volunteers. The purpose for this event is vague and so are the activities. Plausibility cannot be determined. However, the activities appear reactive whereas management as a process suggests a proactive stance is taken to accomplish some given objective(s). Of the four types of functions generally attributed to management (planning, organizing, directing, and controlling), directing seems to be the most overlooked in this and other events.

Event V: Agents Implement Other Program Responsibilities. The purpose of this event is not clear, thus adequacy of activities cannot be judged. However, eight of the eleven activities are organizational rather than programmatic in nature. Placement of plan of work development in this event seems to be out of place in a causal sequence. It is not out of place, however, if plan of work activity is something done to meet organizational responsibility rather than as a programming tool.

6. Resources: An answer to the question of resource adequacy is elusive because it depends on whether one judges adequacy in terms of what is being done or in terms of what someone thinks is needed to be done. It also depends on how effectively present resources are being expended. The resources for the 4-H program are probably adequate (as for any other Extension program) for the present level of participation. More money will probably not increase program effectiveness unless and until changes are made in the program. Stakeholders were split on the question of adequacy: 35% felt the resources were definitely inadequate, 44% felt they were adequate. The others could not decide (6%) or felt no program was adequately funded now (12%). The 4-H state faculty was the only group unanimous in its rating of resources--inadequate. County faculty did not mention this as an area of great concern and volunteers were about evenly split in their perceptions. None of the UM administrators, other Extension faculty, or business leader/state officials groups felt resources were definitely inadequate.

7. Need for Evaluative Information: Persons beyond the level of program implementation were clear about the types of data they would like to have on the program and their needs were realistic. Four-H staff were mostly concerned with descriptive information, e.g., What is the 4-H experience? What happens longitudinally from age 9-19? What are youth and volunteer characteristics? The group of business leader/state officials was mostly interested in who is served by the program, the impact on those served, and if the program was meeting its objectives. University administrators were similarly interested in the audience, especially if the program was working with those who might need it most, and the program's effectiveness but they also wanted information which would be helpful in hiring and keeping faculty--work role, job requirements, and work load.

Recommendations

I.   Define/Clarify the 4-H mission and communicate it to important stakeholders. The mission statement should be specific enough to provide real direction to the program and short enough to be easily understood and communicated. Immediate attention needs to be directed to University administration--the group with probably the greatest potential for directly impacting the statewide 4-H program in Maryland--to educate them about 4-H's mission and to convince them that faculty and volunteers understand and operate in ways to further that mission.

II. Change program efforts and/or program objectives to bring about congruence among intended effects, planned activities, and targeted audience(s). For example, delete adults as target for intended change or add activities to directly impact adults and/or discuss changes in adults as unintended positive outcomes; delete physical and most of the mental effects as intended effects or broaden the activities to increase the probability of their occurrence.

III. If development of life skills is the intended outcome of the 4-H experience,
   a. specify which skills are included,
   b. identify types of experiences that will promote development of each of the skills,
   c. prepare faculty to train volunteers to promote development of these skills,
   d. train volunteers in ways to promote these skills--train all volunteers who work directly with youth--club leaders, project leaders, special interest leaders, etc., and
   e. include life skills content and experiences in each of the projects-- leader manuals and youth manuals--and other 4-H activities.

IV. Define criteria for the minimum 4-H experience in terms of type and number of experiences and/or exposure to subject matter content. Key the criteria to intended effects. Four-H offers a variety of ways a youngster may participate in the program from comprehensive, experientially designed clubs to special interest, short-term groups to day camps to school enrichment classes to TV programs. Will participation in any of these lead to the intended effects? Will any amount of participation lead to the intended effects?

Decide if there is some core of material that everyone considered a 4-H member would have studied, e.g., information about the role of agriculture in the world--on use of natural resources, on food/fiber production cycles, on providing for dietary/clothing/shelter needs, on local/regional economics.

V. Define expectations for the different delivery modes. What experiences should a youngster be assumed to have as a result of participating in a club for some specified period of time? What is expected to go on in the other delivery modes?

VI. Establish a basis for recruiting and selecting volunteers. This could be a function of two sets of criteria: (1) the specific program for the upcoming year, relative to subject matter content, and (2) the specific skills needed to work with youth to obtain intended effects. The present situation seems to consider only or mostly the first set of criteria.

VII. Define the role(s) of volunteers and identify competencies necessary to perform the role(s). Recruit people who demonstrate these competencies and/or provide mandatory training in the desired areas. The rationale for the competencies must be valid and obvious and the training must contribute to volunteer development in these areas. At present, some faculty say volunteers will not participate in training; some volunteers say they get little benefit from attending training sessions.

VIII. Assume a proactive stance in the management of volunteers. One University of Maryland administrator noted this need when he said: "I'm not sure we have provided the leadership for 4-H to be goal directed...Others are providing leadership rather than us,e.g., the volunteers. We don't have to give up our leadership role in order to have participation by clients. ... It takes a special skill to have people involved, participating, and having impact while not dominating. We have a role to provide leadership to make sure that whatever we want to happen, does --we're into leadership, not into service."

IX. Define the job of the 4-H county faculty member and set reasonable expectations for performance. A start was made on this with the Program Model (Appendix II) developed as a part of this evaluability assessment. This model needs to be refined and criteria identified for successful faculty performance.

X. Most of the previous recommendations are predicated on the need for the curriculum of 4-H to be defined, clarified, and made obvious to faculty and other important stakeholders. At present, plan of work development is placed in a causative sequence after other programmatic decisions. It is too costly in time and other resources to be relegated to an organizational maintenance function.

Answers to some of the questions implied in the other recommendations are dependent upon some kind of program plan. For example, questions about mission, about intended effects, about volunteer competence, about faculty role, etc., should all be congruent with one another and that congruence should come from some overriding plan.

ADDENDUM ONE

The logic model of the Maryland 4-H youth program is included as Figure II-1. A description of the activities, performance indicators, and resources follow by individual event.

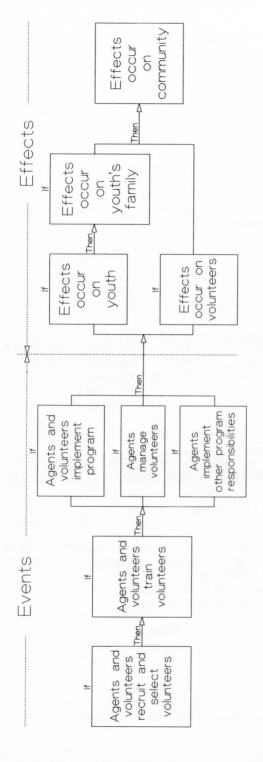

Figure II-1.

ACTIVITIES, PERFORMANCE INDICATORS, AND RESOURCES

I. Agents and Volunteers Recruit and Select Volunteers

Purpose: To secure enough volunteers with appropriate competencies to implement anticipated program with youth.

Activities
1. Continuous informal assessment of number and types of volunteers needed based on upcoming events, number of youth enrolled, and number of new enrollees projected
2. Assign present volunteers to identified tasks
3. Solicit additional volunteers for unfilled roles
   --Secure names of potential volunteers from current volunteers, agencies and organizations (e.g., Volunteer Action Council, PTA), fair exhibits, TV and radio advertisements, and office walk-ins.
   --If any doubt of potential volunteer's fitness to work with youth, conduct individual interview with person; if doubt still persists, get background check by local police department
   --Assign responsibilities
4. Recruitment plan for volunteers for a new club might be as follows:
   --Identify geographic target area based on youth requests for a club there and/or where potential volunteers live and/or where the minority percentage is high and/or where EFNEP or special interest programs are ongoing.
   --Advertise for volunteers in those areas: flyers, posters, articles in community papers.
   --Secure local volunteer to host informational meeting for interested parents and youth.

Indicators/Sources

Presently in place	Could Secure
Letters of acceptance	List of volunteers by tasks
-Letters from community agencies, press clippings, office log	Agent & volunteer self report
-Date of interview on appointment calendar, notes and police report on file	
-Copies of letters to volunteers	
-Minutes of advisory committee meetings	
-Copies of flyers, posters, and news releases news releases	
-Records of attendance	

Resources: 10% of each agents' time: __% of __ volunteers' time; __% of clerical staff time; __$ for posters and other materials.

II. Agents and Volunteers train Volunteers

Purpose: To orient volunteers to 4-H and the Cooperative Extension Service and to prepare them to work with youth to achieve desired effects.

The number and types of volunteers differ from county to county as does the training.   There is no formal curriculum for training volunteers.   Some counties give volunteers a handout which describes youth development, others do not.

Activities
1.   Middle Management or Key Leaders
     --Persons generally have previous experience as 4-H volunteers. Training may be done by agents or other volunteers. It is usually one-on-one and consists of review of
          .4-H mission   .County statistics
          .Tasks to be performed   .Affirmative action guidelines
          .Available resources   .People management
          .Notices of other training opportunities
     --Some counties offer bi-monthly sessions, taught by agents, on topics requested by middle management volunteers, e.g., working with parents, planning programs
     --In some counties, middle management volunteers plan sessions and meet on their own without agent involvement.
2.   Organizational leader for community club
     --Training done by agents or other volunteers. In some counties, the minimum training may be one meeting with the volunteer to plan the first six months' plan for the club. The leader would then be invited to group sessions twice per year on such topics as affirmative action, discipline in meetings, handling competition, and any other topics leaders request.
     --In other counties, agents and/or volunteers will spend one or two individual sessions with the volunteer and cover, either verbally or with a written handout:
          .Role expectations   .Description of 4-H organization
          .Affirmative action guidelines   .County statistics
          .Resources available   .Child development
          .Club guidelines: goals, parliamentary procedure, parent involvement,
               managing money collected by club, interpersonal relationships
          .Notices of group sessions in which leaders may be trained together
     --Agent may attend first club meeting
     --Regional, state, and national training opportunities are advertised to all
          volunteers and in some counties scholarships are provided for one or
          two leaders to attend.
3.   Project leaders (e.g., sewing, pet care).Persons recruited are assumed to have experience in the project areas. Club organization leader usually does the recruiting. Training consists mostly of

--Agreement on number of meetings needed   --Goals of project
--Giving of project manual and   --List of available resources
   leader manual   --Age of enrolled youth
--Notices of county-wide training opportunities

4. Activities/Events leader (e.g., Fashion Revue)
   --Organizational leader describes tasks to be performed and available
   resources
   --Notices provided of county-wide training opportunities

5. Advisory Committee Members. In some counties, information is mailed
   to new members in advance of the first annual meeting. In others, the
   information is presented at the first meeting. Some counties hold new
   member sessions and others orient new members in the presence of carry-
   over members. Other volunteers may assist with the orientation.
   Members are generally "walked through" an advisory manual covering:
   --4-H organization   --Affirmative action guidelines
   --Role/Purpose of committee   --County statistics

6. Judges
   --Sent information by mail on event to be judged
   --Prior to event, agent or volunteer meets with judge in 15- to 30-minute
   session to answer questions
   --Receives notice of training session for judges offered by Maryland
   Association of Fairs

7. Coaches (those who train youth judging teams, bowl teams, etc.)
   --Agent and/or other volunteer meets with person to set up schedule,
   review previous team's weaknesses, pan what to teach, and give handout
   on coaching

8. Fair Volunteers. Training is done by another volunteer and is mostly
   verbal descriptions of
   --Department at fair   --Classes to be offered
   --How to process entries   --How to select judges
   --Recording results   --Managing parents and youth
   --Displaying exhibits   --Public relations
   --Awards, trophies

9. Agents may assist with volunteer training in other counties and states.

Indicators/Sources

Presently in place	Could Secure
Lesson plans	Agent, leader-trainers, and
Notices of meetings in newsletters, newspapers	volunteer self reports
Date of training on appointment	Leader tests of knowledge
calendar of agents	about 4-H, CES, and life
Copies of handouts	skills development
Attendance records	
Copies of letters to volunteers	

Resources: 25% of each agents' time; 1 day per year per volunteer; 5 different
printed handouts per year; 2-3 state specialist days per county per year
Community agencies: 2 person days per year; $1,000 to $2,000 per agent

III. Agents and Volunteers Implement Program

Purpose: To carry out events/activities to achieve intended audience effects.

In some counties volunteers do essentially all tasks related to implementing the program; in other counties, agents do many of the tasks.

Activities
1. Recruit youth
   --Agents design and print posters, flyers, book marks, etc. and secure others from state 4-H office. Volunteers disseminate these in designated areas.
   --Agents, with volunteer assistance, design/develop/set up/man exhibits for shopping malls, schools, public libraries, and other public places.
   --Volunteer and/or agents make presentations to community service clubs.
   --Agents (occasionally volunteers) create articles for newspaper and radio and newsletters of other groups like Extension Homemakers, PTA News, school newsletter.
   --Agents make presentations at school enrichment on what, when, where of 4-H activities; send followup to teachers with invitations for specific events/activities
   --4-H members are asked to invite others to participate.
2. Agents plan affirmative action activities, volunteers assist with implementation.
3. Solicit donations: Agents write letters to potential donors; volunteers assist with mailing tasks.
4. Agents and/or volunteers hold county-wide project area workshops which are open to anyone.
5. Agents present more in-depth special interest workshops, open to anyone.
6. Secure Resources: Volunteers (occasionally agents) order project manuals and other materials and arrange for speakers and facilities.
7. Organizational leaders plan six-months to year in advance and submit plans to agents.
8. Volunteers assist other volunteers with any problems. The agent is contacted if they cannot resolve them alone.
9. Volunteers (occasionally agents) visit clubs for informal evaluation of how well leaders are implementing activities in terms of assigned responsibilities.
10. Volunteers judge project books.
11. Assess needs of youth in specific county: Some counties indicate that local needs assessment is a part of their programming; other insist that the project nature of the 4-H curriculum precludes 4-H's ability to respond to local needs. Where needs are assessed, activities include:

--Agents sometimes ask advisory committees for input

--Agents study written data, e.g., newspaper articles, U. S. Census, report from Governor's Council on Status of Youth, Specialists' reports, and Maryland Department of Agriculture reports

--Agents serve on other community committees and participate in discussions of youth needs.

--Volunteers informally make input on youth needs

Indicators/Sources

Presently in place	Could Secure
--Copies of materials produced,	--Agent and Volunteer self report
--Exhibits	--Pictures of exhibits
--Letters of invite, "thank you"	--Service club member reports
	--Minutes of club meetings
--News releases and press clippings	--Copies of newsletters
--Copies of letters	--Teachers' and students'reports
--Affirmative Action Reports	--Committee member reports
--Record books of clubs	--Membership lists and attendance
--Lesson plans, attendance records	records of community committees
--Copies of order forms	
--Copies of leader plans	
--Visits noted on appointment calendars.	
--Copies of judging forms	
--Advisory committee meeting minutes	
--Copies of data/information considered	

Resources

Agents: __ FTE; Volunteers: 15 days per volunteer per year;
Written material per youth per year: Approximately 50 different handouts

IV. Agents Manage Volunteers

Purpose: To assist volunteers in whatever ways necessary to get the activities successfully implemented.

Activities
1. Prepare newsletter for volunteers, six to eight times per year, covers announcements of upcoming events, tips, recognition for work done, etc.
2. Prepare newsletter for youth, six to ten times per year.
3. Develop/Adapt curriculum materials
4. Answer volunteer questions
5. Motivate volunteers by making phone calls, attending events with them, and just being available to listen.
6. Assist with securing resources, e.g., contact agencies, specialists, etc.
7. Coordinate special interest, school enrichment, and EFNEP activities. Contact sponsors and teach classes or arrange for others to.
8. Attend advisory committee meetings, fair board meetings, and county-wide activity meetings.
9. Keep records of enrollments, affirmative action efforts, program plans, number of volunteers worked with, leader briefs, etc.
10. Provide recognition for adults and youth. Secure awards, secure speakers, script program, and assist with program.
11. Alert as to upcoming events.

Indicators/Sources
Presently in place   Could secure
--Copies of newsletters and materials   --Self reports by persons involved
--Copies of correspondence
--Travel records, appointments
--Lesson plans
--Minutes of meetings
--Records in file
--Copies of programs, letters, bills for awards

Resources: 35% of each agents' time;   Printed materials: 15-20 handouts per volunteer; $5,000 - $8,000 per agent (does not include county fair expenses)

V. Agents Implement Other Program Responsibilities

Purpose: To develop/refine agent personal capabilities and to maintain the CES organization such that planned program activities can occur.

Activities
1. Monthly: Prepare time and contact reports, attend county faculty meetings
2. Every two to six months: attend county EAC meetings
3. Annually
   --Prepare curriculum vitae
   --Write narrative accomplishment reports on two key Plan of Work sub programs
   --Prepare two-page annual report of accomplishments
4. Develop Plan of Work
   --Gather data on county situation
   --Gather data on other 4-H programs within/out county
   --Determine youth potential for county
   --Decide programming and evaluation activities for specified period
5. Prepare expense vouchers as needed
6. Participate on other youth boards in county
7. Participate in professional development activities
8. Serve on state 4-H committees and task forces
9. Manage clerical staff and summer work students. (Some agents also assist with recruiting and hiring clerical staff).
10. Chaperone youth to county, state, and national events--sometimes with volunteer assistance
11. Serve as judge for events in other counties
12. Write letters of recommendation for youth and volunteers

Indicators/Sources
Presently in place	Could secure
--Copies of reports, minutes, and other prepared documents	--Youth board member reports and and minutes of meetings
	--Agent reports
--Letters of authorization	--Agent and trainer reports
--Letters of appointment and "thank you"	--State specialist reports
--Annual evaluation forms on staff and students	--Agent, staff, clerical assistants self reports
--Travel records	--Agent, youth, volunteer self ----
Notations on appointment caldendars	reports
--Copies of letters	

Resources
   30% of each agents' time
   30% of one clerical staff members' time

VI. Effects Occur on Youth

Effects
1. Acquire knowledge in
    --Project content areas
    --Parliamentary procedure
    --Officer responsibilities
    --Careers
    --Record keeping and business skills
    --Decision making process
2. Acquire new skills
    --Communication
    --Leadership
    --Getting along with others
    --Citizenship
    --Goal setting
    --Project area skills, e.g., woodworking
3. Learn about community and how to change it
4. Improved self esteem
5. Increased employability skills
6. Experience with adults other than parents and teachers
7. Exchange club members acquire knowledge of other peoples and cultures

Indicators/Sources

Presently in place	Could Secure
--Record books	--Pre/post knowledge tests
	--Observation of public
	speeches and demonstrations
	--Correct answers in academic bowl
	--Youth, Leader, family member
	reports
--Copies of news articles, radio	--Parent, teacher, peer reports
scripts written by youth; public	--Reports by club members
speeches and demonstrations	--List of Projects completed from
--Thank you letters from community	--Youth and community members'
groups	reports;
--Goals written in record books	--List of community projects
--Judges' evaluations of record books	projects in which participated
and project-related competitive	--Attendance at community
events	meetings
--Products completed in projects	--List of jobs attained

VII. Effects Occur on Volunteers

Effects
1. Acquire knowledge in
    --Program planning
    --County statistics
    --Group management
    --Community resources
    --Record keeping
    --Club officer roles/responsibilities
    --Decision making process
    --Project content
2. Improve skills
    --Writing
    --Management
    --Public speaking
    --Record keeping
    --Leadership
3. Increase feelings of self worth
4. Increase employability

Indicators/Sources

Presently in place
--Copies of program plans
--Program plans cite county statistics
--Evaluation forms completed by
    youth, parents, & other volunteers
--Program plans include wide range
    of community resources
--Copies of records
--New releases printed by papers
--Copies of letters, records
    --Evaluation forms completed by
      youth, parents, & other volunteers

Could Secure
--Before and after knowledge tests
--Volunteer self reports
--Employability records--jobs held
  prior to 4-H experience and those
  held after

VIII. Effects Occur on Family of 4-H Members

Effects
1. Acquire knowledge in project areas
2. Increase feelings of pride for 4-H'ers accomplishments
3. Family members do more things together and communicate more

Indicators/Sources
    Presently in place

                                      Could Secure
                                        --Pre-post project knowledge tests
                                        --Reports by family members
                                        --Reports by family members

IX. Effects Occur on Community

Effects
1. Increase in number of volunteers doing community work
2. Community groups get services, e.g., 4-H'ers serve food baskets to the elderly, clean up and fix up public property
3. People in community become more aware of some of its minorities, e.g., handicapped, and other special groups like latch-key kids
4. Community is safer as a result of programs like bicycle safety

Indicators/Sources

Presently in place	Could Secure
--Letters of request and "thank you"	--Reports by agencies and city/county government
--Club reports	--Before/After pictures
--News articles	--Reports by community groups
	--Content analysis of local newspapers for stories on minorities--before 4-H projects and after
	--Police reports of number of accidents in communities before and after 4-H programs on safety

Evaluability Assessment of the
Local Government Officials Program
Illinois Cooperative Extension Service
Charles D. Clark and M. F. Smith*

Introduction

The evaluability assessment (EA) was undertaken to aid the planning of an evaluation of the Illinois Extension programs for local government officials. Specifically it was hoped that the evaluability assessment would meet the following objectives:

1) Identify those programs or program elements which were sufficiently developed to be likely to produce impact in terms of changes in knowledge, skills, or abilities and/or economic and/or social benefits.
2) Suggest how a study might be designed to measure such impact.
3) Identify the utility of an impact type evaluation in meeting the information needs of key administrators.
4) Determine the extent of support for such an impact evaluation.

A review of program documents, interviews with stakeholders, and development of a model of program operation were used to meet these objectives.

Procedures

This section reports the steps followed in conducting the evaluability assessment and discusses limitations of the procedures. The steps followed included identification of and bounding the subject of the evaluation, formation of an evaluation planning committee, collection of data, and development of a model of program operations.

Bounding the Program

The initial charge for the impact evaluation was to conduct an evaluation of Extension's educational programs for local government officials.

*Clark is Program Evaluation Specialist, Illinois Cooperative Extension Service, University of Illinois, Urbana; Smith is Associate Professor and Coordinator, Program Planning and Evaluation, Cooperative Extension Service, University of Maryland, College Park.

As with previous impact evaluations planned in Illinois, responsibility for the evaluation rested with the assistant director(s) associated with the subject matter area. Great latitude has been exercised concerning the scope of such evaluations.

All subject matter specialists and area advisers conducting programs with public officials as a principle audience reviewed their programs with the assistant director, the state evaluation specialist and the outside resource team* supporting the evaluability assessment. During these meetings the nature of impact evaluations was reviewed with the state specialists and area advisers. Several felt that an impact study was inappropriate for their efforts because they already knew their program activities were not sufficient to produce desired impact and/or conditions were such that it seemed unlikely that information collected through an evaluation would be used to improve the program.

The program finally selected for the evaluability assessment was County Board Member TeleNets. (TeleNet refers to the Illinois Cooperative Extension Service's two-way teleconferencing network.) In addition to other factors considered, the enthusiasm of the program staff for the EA and possible followup indepth evaluation weighed heavily in the decision. This selection bounded the focus of the assessment by both the audience served and the delivery technique.

Description of the Program

The County Board TeleNets Programs are part of the Illinois Cooperative Extension Service's involvement in the Community Information and Education Service (CIES). CIES is a cooperative venture by Extension, the University of Illinois Office of Continuing Education and Public Service, and five central Illinois Community Colleges. It was initiated in 1980 with a multi-year grant by the W. K. Kellogg Foundation. These special funds were to continue until the middle of 1986. CIES's stated purpose is to "provide information and educational assistance to public officials, civic organizations, planning groups, and the general public...on locally identified community issues" (1984 CIES Annual Report).

County Board TeleNet programs began in 1982 using Extension's TeleNet system. TeleNet is a dedicated audio teleconferencing system with 115 remote sites statewide. During 1984, five programs for county board members were delivered. Topics included county jails, collective bargaining, orientation for newly elected board members, and financial and personnel management. During 1984, two-thirds (65) of the state's counties participated in the programs.

County Extension faculty (agents) participate in planning the programs, marketing the programs to their county boards, insuring the -

---

*Dr. M. F. Smith, Coordinator, Program Planning and Evaluation, CES, University of Maryland and Dr. George Mayeske, Program Evaluation Specialist, Extension Service, USDA.

availability of program materials, and hosting the programs at Extension county offices.

Planning Committee Members

Members of the EA planning committee were:

o The Assistant Director for Community Resource Development and Co-director for the CIES project.
o A Resource Specialist from the Office of Continuing Education and Public Service with responsibilities for CIES.
o An Area Extension Adviser with community education responsibilities.
o An Extension Assistant with community resource responsibilities.
o The TeleNet System Coordinator.
o The Extension Specialist for Program Evaluation.
o The two outside evaluability assessment consultants.

Four of the Illinois committee members had responsibilities directly related to the delivery of the TeleNet programs. The exceptions were the Assistant Director and the evaluation specialist. Guidance and assistance in development of the procedures was provided by the two outside EA consultants: Smith and Mayeske.

Data Collection

Data collection consisted of interviews with stakeholders, analysis of program documents, and discussions with the planning group.

Selection of the stakeholders to be interviewed and the development of the interview schedules was done by the planning committee. Those interviewed were the members of the planning committee, two county extension advisers, the Director and Associate Director of Extension, the Dean of the College of Agriculture, the Continuing Education Co-director for the CIES project, and the Associate Vice Chancellor for Continuing Education and Public Service.

All interviews were conducted by the Illinois Extension program evaluation specialist. Transcribed interview notes were reviewed and confirmed by the interviewees.

Interviews were conducted with the two county extension advisers primarily to confirm the priority which county staff were suspected to have regarding program objectives. These interviews also served as a check on model operation. Anonymity was provided the two county advisers.

Interviews with administrators began with a general inquiry regarding objectives for the CIES project and then focused on the objectives of the

County Board TeleNets. Interviews with the state and area program staff focused on objectives and needs assessment information.

With regard to program activities, administrators were asked a general question about what activities they expected program staff to perform. Program and county staff were questioned more closely about activities, working relationships and barriers to program implementation. Both groups were asked similar questions about program resource adequacy.

Many of the interviews focused on evaluation of the program. Administrators were asked about the current sources of information they use for monitoring program performance and their interest in additional or more formal evaluation. Questions also focused on the timing and reporting of such evaluations. Program staff were asked about their feelings regarding such an evaluation, outcomes the evaluation might attempt to measure, and how they might use such information to influence decisions. Results of the interviews are presented in the next section. Program documents reviewed by the Illinois evaluation specialist included annual reports for the CIES project, funding proposals, completed evaluations for the County Board TeleNets, and TeleNet promotion materials. Also reviewed were documents developed on the use of two-way audio teleconferencing and the TeleNet system.

Program Model Development

The initial version of the program operations model was developed with the assistance of the outside EA consultants. Several iterations ensued with the Illinois evaluation specialist circulating each version to committee members and making revisions during group interviews.

Following completion of the interviews with stakeholders, the committee reviewed the summaries of the interviews under the leadership of Dr. Smith and developed a final detailed model of program operations (Addendum One).

Potential Limitations of Procedures

One of the potential limitations of this EA was the small number of interviewees, e.g., only two county Extension advisers were interviewed. The greatest potential oversight was not including representatives of the Kellogg Foundation--a primary funder--and the five community colleges.

These omissions are viewed as a "potential" limitation because even though important information may have been gained, it would have come at a cost--and we are not sure of what the net result would have been. For example, adding more interviewees would have required additional interviewers which would have extended the time necessary to complete the study--and time was of the essence since this program was supported by outside funds that were about to expire.

Interviewer bias could have entered into the study but attempts were made to identify where these might occur and steps were taken to overcome them. Having one interviewer helped--since any bias should have been consistent across all interviews. Also, all interviewees, with the exception of one, were provided transcripts of the original interviews and given opportunity to make corrections or editorial changes.

Discussion of Findings

Plausibility of Impact

Agreement on Goals

From the interviews, it appears that there is agreement that the program is to produce changes in knowledge and skill among a specific target audience: county board members; it is not clear how many board members from how many counties would constitute success. The priority this goal appears to receive varies with county Extension advisers giving higher priority to what administrators tend to see as only a side benefit, that of increasing county board support. However, both goals are acknowledged by both groups.

There was less agreement on other goals. A variety of possible outcomes were mentioned when staff were questioned about goals and the outcomes which an evaluation might address.

Adequacy of Program Activities

Some evidence (primarily through self-reports by board members through telephone interviews) suggests that the TeleNets have been effective in meeting board member educational needs. However, there may be some areas of program implementation deserve a closer monitoring to help insure that the agreed upon goal is met. Among these are the level of organizational commitment and human resource commitment to the program; the availability of unbiased, qualified resource persons; the adequacy of program promotion; and the effectiveness of using one medium to bring about the program objectives.

Two concerns related to organizational and human resource commitment (Step 1 in the Model,) were raised in the interviews. One was whether Cooperative Extension would be able to maintain staff involved in the programs due to changes in funding levels and expiration of the Kellogg grant. The other was the extent to which local government officials were legitimate audiences for extension programs.

Identification of resource persons to address emerging issues (Step 4 in Model) appeared to be of concern to some administrators and program staff. Such concerns were reflected in the need to guard against bias and the need to interest researchers in county government problems.

Promotion and implementation of the County Board TeleNets are dependent upon the efforts of county extension advisers (Step 6 in Model). One of the concerns in working relationships was that some county advisers may not be adequately promoting the programs. Additional concerns were raised about charging fees for the programs.

Measurability of Impact Indicators

Directions for Design of a Study

The model lists performance indicators which were identified by the evaluation planning committee and the resource team. These are measurable at what appears to be reasonable cost. What has not been developed are ·standards to indicate the level of performance which would indicate adequate implementation or impact.

Who Wants What Information, When, and in What form

Highest priority among administrators favoring additional evaluation was a case study focusing on what has been learned from the cooperative venture among Extension, Continuing Education, and community colleges. Evaluative information was also seen as useful in continued program development. Administrators rely upon the level of program participation, participant reactions, and staff reports as their primary sources of information.

Program staff tended to favor data which would influence administrators. Evaluative data were also seen as important for program development, for county adviser acceptance of programs, and for maintaining and increasing resource commitments to the program.

Evaluative information was needed within six to twelve months to influence funding and staffing decisions, although a continuous flow was requested by some administrators and program planners. Administrators tended to prefer short, executive summaries backed up by more formal, extensive reports.

Conclusions

The program appears adequate to produce changes in county board members' knowledge--an objective for which there is widespread agreement. There are portions of the program's operation which could be strengthened to improve the probability this objective is being reached. Additional efforts may be necessary to increase the number of counties and board members participating in the programs.

Level of participation and participant reactions appear to be the primary outcome indicators being utilized by both administrators and program staff. Some administrators consider this, with staff reports, to be adequate. Administrators differ in the emphasis they would give to a more formal, impact evaluation. Program staff, as a group, appear to be more interested in such a study than do administrators. There is broad support from

Extension administrators for a case study to identify the elements which contributed to the success of the cooperative nature of the TeleNets and the overall CIES program.

Impact of Evaluability Assessment

Since the evaluability assessment was conducted several changes have taken place:

1. A staff member who had previously been on special project funds and had been placed on a "terminal" contract has been moved to more regular funds with the responsibilities of an area adviser in Local Government Education. This extension staff member continues to work with county board TeleNets.

2. Additional funding has been secured from the Kellogg Foundation to continue the CIES project with some alterations. Among other things this funding is being used to:
    a. contract with local government experts who will research, develop and deliver a core curriculum to officials,
    b. develop professionally designed program materials,
    c. provide training to upgrade faculty skills in distance teaching.

3. Changes have been made to improve the promotion and delivery of the program by local Extension staff.

4. A variation of the program is now being used with the Office of Continuing Education and community colleges to extend the content to a wider audience--municipal officials.

ADDENDUM ONE

The logic model of the Illinois Local Government Officials Program is included as Figure III-1.

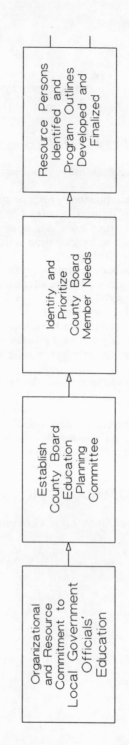

Figure III-1.

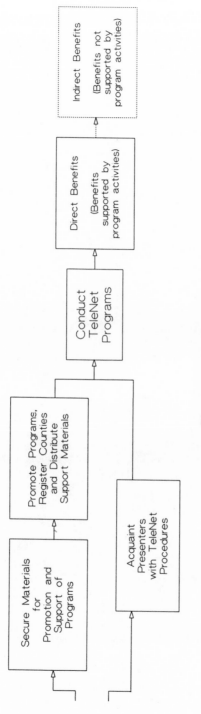

Figure III-1. Continued.

Evaluability Assessment of the
Master Gardener Program
California Cooperative Extension
Dennis Pittenger, James J. Grieshop, and M. F. Smith*

Introduction and Background on Program

From a start in 1978 in Washington, the Cooperative Extension's Master Gardener (MG) program has blossomed into maturity in more than 35 states. The program utilizes volunteers at the county level who conduct educational programs that meet gardening needs of local residents. They provide an organized approach to demands for information and problem-solving help. In exchange for as many as 50 hours of organized horticultural instruction from extension and other professionals, the volunteers teach, organize, support, and do a variety of jobs that enhance the local community and Cooperative Extension programs. In California, the Master Gardener program has been an active one, growing from two programs to over 20 in less than four years. First test piloted in 1980, the lessons learned about development and organizational problems helped to rapidly diffuse the program to 20 additional counties by the end of 1984. This spread occurred with limited statewide coordination. Counties generally determined their own program organization, activities and subject matter content.

Throughout this process, appropriate and common extension practices (i.e., need identification, use of advisory groups, pilot demonstrations, monitoring and diffusion strategy) were employed. However, full-scale evaluation of California's programs had not been sufficiently addressed. Many concerns about the program casually expressed in recent years by extension educators (e.g., is it solving problems, does it use too many resources) all helped to create a climate for considering the question of evaluation.

Concerns centered on the use of resources, how the program could be improved, and where the program was headed. Most questions were directed to Urban Horticulture Specialist Dennis Pittenger who had the most central involvement in the program statewide. Previous evaluation efforts had largely focused on the impact of the program on volunteers and program activity data. Neither detailed analyses of program activity data nor detailed analyses of the program or its direction were available. Despite interest in

*Pittenger is Urban Horticulture Specialist, and Grieshop, Specialist in Community Education, Cooperative Extension, University of California, Davis. Smith is Associate Professor and Coordinator, Program Planning and Evaluation, Cooperative Extension Service, University of Maryland, College Park.

more of an in-depth evaluation by Pittenger, sufficient expertise was not readily available to help determine whether a detailed evaluation effort was appropriate.   At the same time, Assistant Director for Planning and Evaluation, Doris Smith, aware of the specialist's dilemma, was presented with an opportunity to become involved in an EA case study. The MG program in all twenty (plus) counties in which it was operating at the time of the EA, was selected as the focus.

Select a Working Team

Once it was clear that the MG program was a potential case study candidate, a team was assembled to carry it out. This team consisted of two county master gardener advisors, two state specialists, the Assistant Director for Cooperative Extension and two resource people from the EA project. County advisors were selected because they were both interested in program evaluation and had conducted MG programs. The two specialists included the one that was responsible for the MG program becoming established in the state and the one currently involved in its operation.

The team's expectations for the EA can be best visualized in terms of individual, programmatic and organizational perspectives. Individually, they wanted (and expected) to learn more about evaluability assessment and the evaluation process in general. Programmatically, it was anticipated that a clearer understanding of the Master Gardener program and measures of its impacts would emerge. From the organizational view, the expectation was to determine whether or not EA had the potential to become a practical component of extension evaluation procedures.   At the outset, it was presumed that the entire EA process would be completed within six months, with a maximum of 25 work days involved.

Procedure

The Master Gardener EA was carried out over a period of six months beginning in April and finishing in late September, 1985. The primary work was carried out by the workgroup composed of seven persons supplemented by two part-time graduate student researchers, with input from four county-based Cooperative Extension personnel.

The work process consisted of a series of one- and two-day workgroup consultations held in mid-April, mid-July, and late-September. In between, individual members conducted work projects, principally interviewing and performing analyses of interview results and specifying the emerging Master Gardener program model.

April 10-11, 1985, Consultation

The initial meeting of the workgroup was held in Riverside, California, and initiated by Drs. Midge Smith and George Mayeske. Their intent was to use the California MG program as one case for the EA process. The first meeting was to review a Draft Manual for EA and, more importantly, to develop the commitment needed to become fully engaged to carry out the project.

A variety of tasks were undertaken. Stakeholders were identified and a schedule established for conducting their interviews. Revision of the proposed questions for administrative, operational and volunteer stakeholders was accomplished. The meetings also served to establish the necessary targets and to agree upon the common strategy. Because of the limited time available and the urgency to complete the project, the workgroup agreed to utilize graduate students to work with specialists and the Assistant Director also agreed to conduct interviews. June 30 was established as the target for completing the interviews.

Forty-three stakeholders were identified to be interviewed: Director of Cooperative Extension, the Associate Director for Programs, the Director of Communication Programs, Program directors in Vegetable Crops and Environmental Horticulture/Pomology, two Regional Directors, four County Directors, three County Advisors responsible for the management of Master Gardener programs, 26 MG volunteers, and three elected officials.

April - May - June, 1985 -Conduct Interviews

In late-April, contacts were made with interviewees. The first interview was carried out on May 1st and all were completed by mid-June. The MG volunteers were interviewed by telephone, following a structured list of questions. All other interviews were carried out in person; most were tape recorded. Each interview used the set of questions designed for each category of stakeholders, i.e., the administrators, the operators of the program, and the volunteers in the program. Interviews were designed to collect qualitative data as to views of the program, impacts, activities, and desired evaluation data.

During the course of the interviews, several minor problems emerged. (1) Specific wording of some interview questions created a lack of "shared meaning." That is, designers of the questions often had one meaning for such words as "evaluation," "goal," or "problems," whereas the interviewees often times had significantly different meanings. One case serves to illustrate. A question asked of the MG volunteers was the type of problems they faced as they were involved in the program. From the point of view of the question writers, the problems referred to management problems in the operation of the program. However, Master Gardeners interpreted "problems" to mean what kind of horticultural problems they faced. A continuous process of rephrasing questions resulted. (2) Several of the stakeholders interviewed should not have been. This was particularly true in the case of the political stakeholders, who had never heard of the program.

July 24-25, 1985, Consultation - Review Interviews and construct logic model

The work team met again in July to consider the interview data and to construct the Master Gardener program "logic." Components of the logic were identified and a model configuration constructed. During these two days, a full measure of discussion, evaluation, and reflection occurred. These activities in turn led to a clear understanding of the logic of the MG program.

It is very difficult to adequately convey, by writing, the energy and concentration needed to construct the logic (of the program). Discussion and interaction are vital elements since the process involved is one of developing shared understandings and meanings of concepts such as the "Master Gardener program," "evaluation goals," "impacts," "activities" and "indicators." In fact, more time should have been dedicated, both at this point and each of the other two consultation points to building consensus.

Before concluding the July consultation, it was decided to meet again as a group in late-September to take the final steps of verification and validation of the program logic and to decide whether or not to carry out a full-scale evaluation.

August-September, 1985

During August and September, Dr. Midge Smith and Dr. George Mayeske reduced the mass of raw and slightly processed data to construct the logic of the MG program. They fitted identified activities and indicators of activities to key events in a logical programming framework. Other members of the work group for this period of time were more or less unencumbered with having to deal with week-to-week thoughts of the Master Gardener EA.

September 26, 1985, Consultation

The third consultation was held to review, revise, modify, and verify the written program logic. The process involved a review of interview materials, recollections of earlier discussions, the continued clarification of primary terms, and the clarification of activities and indicators. The complete program model is included in Addendum 1.

An important feature of this consultation was the presence of four California Cooperative Extension professionals who were asked, over a three-hour period, to review the proposed logic and to verify and validate the logic. An item-by-item review process of the written logic, with adequate attempts to question and clarify points mentioned and as well to add, was used. In the time allotted, these "validators" were able to ask specific questions that added immeasurably to the logic description. The four validators who had not been previously interviewed and were unfamiliar with the EA, were involved with Master Gardener programs. Although difficult to judge whether or not it would have been better to have persons previously interviewed as validators, these "newcomers" to the process seemed to add considerably to the outcome.

Again, it is difficult to describe the intensity involved in a one-day meeting. There probably was not enough time to adequately address some concerns.

Conclusions and Next Steps

October, 1985, Post-Consultation

At the end of the consultation, the important questions of what to do with the logic and whether or not an evaluation should be carried out, were confronted. A tentative conclusion was that a full-scale evaluation of the California Master Gardener program was premature. A more definitive answer had to await a third review of the interviews, focused principally on what stakeholders expected to receive from an evaluation. In this postconsultation period, it was concluded that no compelling reasons to conduct an evaluation currently existed. The EA indicated that certain key stakeholders would be indifferent to evaluation results. Thus, the EA revealed no valid and compelling reason to conduct a programmatic evaluation.

Although the major expectations for the EA were met and no evaluation is called for, there are some next steps. Particularly important is the suggestion to develop a greater consensus within the organization as to the role of the Master Gardener program. Although the organization's view of the MG program is that of an information/dissemination program, it is much more. The MG program is a problem-solving one and, in reality, no different from any other extension education program.

Although a decision has been made not to conduct an evaluation, understanding of the Master Gardening program has been immeasurably improved--its ambiguities, its strengths, and its weaknesses are now much more visible. It is now quite clear that additional time and effort must be addressed to clarifying the goals and activities, leadership training, and the overall management of the program. Available data and results can now be used to discuss these conclusions with Program Directors and other stakeholders. The EA can be used as a first step for building the necessary consensus. Finally, since an EA attempts to reconcile rhetoric with reality, those involved must be very clear in meanings of words (for example, goals or problems). These have to be expressed very clearly in discussing or questioning the goals and management of the program.

Addendum One

The logic model of the California Cooperative Extension master gardener program is included in Figure IV-1.

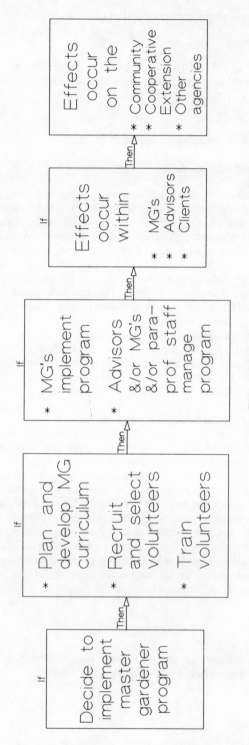

Figure IV-1.

References Cited

Anderson, C. M. 1981. Self-Image therapy. In R. J. Corsini (ed.), HANDBOOK OF INNOVATIVE PSYCHOTHERAPIES. New York: Wiley.

ASKSAM. 1986. Version 3. Seaside Software, Inc. Perry, Florida.

Barry, B. and Rae, D. W. 1975. Political evaluation. In F. I. Greenstein and N. W. Plosby (eds.), HANDBOOK OF POLITICAL SCIENCE, Vol. 1. Reading, MA: Addison-Wesley.

Bennett, C. F. 1979. ANALYZING IMPACTS OF EXTENSION PROGRAMS. U.S. Department of Agriculture, Science and Education Administration. ESC-575.

Berk, Richard A. 1981. On the Compatibility of Applied and Basic Sociological Research: An Effort in Marriage Counseling. THE AMERICAN SOCIOLOGIST, Vol. 16: 204-211.

Bickman, L. 1987a. The functions of program theory. In L. Bickman (ed.) USING PROGRAM THEORY IN EVALUATION. New Directions for Program Evaluation, No. 33. San Francisco: Jossey-Bass.

Bickman, L. (ed.) 1987b. USING PROGRAM THEORY IN EVALUATION. New Directions for Program Evaluation, No. 33. San Francisco: Jossey-Bass.

Bocialetti, G. and Kaplan R.E. 1986. "Self-study" for human services agencies: Managing a three-sided relationship. EVALUATION AND PROGRAM PLANNING, Vol. 9(1): 1-11.

Boyle, P. G. 1981. PLANNING BETTER PROGRAMS. New York: McGraw-Hill.

Bradburn, N. M. 1982. Question-wording effects in surveys. In R. M. Hogarth (ed.) QUESTION FRAMING AND RESPONSE CONSISTENCY. San Francisco: Jossey-Bass.

Brannon, E. L., Evans, D. and Rush, F. 1987. Extension's small home-based business programming in Alabama: An evaluability assessment. Unpublished study. Auburn, AL: Alabama Cooperative Extension Service.

Bredo, E., and Feinberg, W. 1982. KNOWLEDGE AND VALUES IN SOCIAL AND EDUCATIONAL RESEARCH. Philidelphia: Temple University Press.

Burry, J. 1973. R and D in education: Foundations for evaluation. UCLA EDUCATOR, 15 (Winter): 14-16.

Cameron, K. 1980. Critical questions in assessing organizational effectiveness. ORGANIZATIONAL DYNAMICS, Vol. 9: 66-80.

Cantwell, R. M. 1985. A note on the potential for bias in the structure and wording of questionnaire items. EVALUATION NEWS, Vol. 6(2): 9-15.

Caulley, D. N. 1983. Document analysis in program evaluation. EVALUATION AND PROGRAM PLANNING, Vol. 6: 19-29.

Champion, H. 1985. Physician heal thyself: One public manager's view of program evaluation. EVALUATION NEWS, Vol. 6(1): 29-40.

Chen, H. T. and Rossi, P. H. 1983. Evaluating with sense, The theory driven approach. EVALUATION REVIEW, Vol. 7(3): 283-302.

Clark, C. C. 1987. Report of an evaluability assessment of Illinois local government officials education county board telenets. Impact Study Report IL94IS, University of Illinois, Urbana Illinois Cooperative Extension Service.

Cook, T. D. and Campbell, D. T. 1979. QUASI-EXPERIMENTATION, DESIGN AND ANALYSIS ISSUES FOR FIELD SETTINGS. Chicago: Rand McNally.

Cook, T. D., Leviton, L. C., and Shadish, Jr., W. R. 1985. Program evaluation. In G. Lindzey and E. Aronson (eds.) HANDBOOK OF SOCIAL PSYCHOLOGY (3rd edition) New York: Random House.

Conrad, K. J. and Miller, T. Q. 1987. Measuring and testing program philosophy. In L. Bickman (ed.) USING PROGRAM THEORY IN EVALUATION. New Directions for Program Evaluation, No. 33. San Francisco: Jossey-Bass.

Cronbach, L. J. and Associates. 1980. TOWARD REFORM OF PROGRAM EVALUATION. San Francisco: Jossey-Bass.

de Geus, A. P. 1988. Planning and Learning. HARVARD BUSINESS REVIEW. March-April.

Dillman, D. 1978. MAIL AND TELEPHONE SURVEYS. New York: Wiley & Sons.

Drucker, P. F. 1967. THE EFFECTIVE EXECUTIVE. New York: Harper and Row. In EXECUTIVE SUMMARY PROGRAM. 1986. Vol. 2(2): 2-8. MacMillan Book Clubs, Inc.

Dunn, W. N., Mitroff, I. I., and Deutsch, S. J. 1981. The obsolescence of evaluation research. EVALUATION AND PROGRAM PLANNING, Vol. 4(3-4): 207-218.

Edelman, M. 1977. POLITICAL LANGUAGE: WORDS THAT SUCCEED AND POLICIES THAT FAIL. New York: Academic Press.

Eichelberger, R. T. 1986. Interview with Jeff Schiller: A "dinosaur" in federal govenment evaluation. EVALUATION PRACTICE, Vol. 7(3): 25-34.

Eisner, E. W. 1979. THE EDUCATIONAL IMAGINATION. New York: MacMillan.

EMPLOYMENT AND TRAINING REPORTER. 1982. Vol. 13: 831.

EVALUATION NEWS. 1985. Vol. 6(3): 44.

Farley, J. 1987. Justifying conclusions in naturalistic evaluations: A practical perspective. EVALUATION AND PROGRAM PLANNING, 10(4): 343-350.

Frankfather, D. 1984. The value of unattractive characteristics in social entitlements. EVALUATION AND PROGRAM PLANNING, Vol. 7(3): 291-299.

Freeman, H. E. and Solomon, M. A. 1981. Introduction: Evaluation and the uncertain '80's. In EVALUATION STUDIES REVIEW ANNUAL. Beverly Hills: Sage.

FYI 3000 PLUS. 1987. Austin, Texas: FYI, Inc.

Gentry, D. L. 1981. Brief therapy I. In R. J. Corsini (ed.) HANDBOOK OF INNOVATIVE PSYCHOTHERAPIES. New York: Wiley.

Glenwick, D. S., Stephens, M. A. P., and Maher, C. A. 1984. On considering the unintended impact of evaluation: Reactive distortions in program goals and activities. EVALUATION AND PROGRAM PLANNING, Vol. 7(4): 321-327.

Greene, J. C. 1987a. Justifying conclusions in naturalistic evaluations: A practical perspective. EVALUATION AND PROGRAM PLANNING, Vol. 10(4): 325-333.

Greene, J. C. 1987b. Stakeholder paricipation in evaluation design: Is it worth the effort? EVALUATION AND PROGRAM PLANNING, Vol. 10(4): 379-394.

Gross, B. M. 1968. ORGANIZATIONS AND THEIR MANAGING. New York: The Free Press.

Guba, E. G. and Lincoln, Y. S. 1981. EFFECTIVE EVALUATION. San Francisco: Jossey-Bass.

Halberstam, D. 1979. THE POWERS THAT BE. New York: Alfred A. Knopf.

Hendricks, M. 1984. Finis. President's corner. EVALUATION NEWS, Vol. 5(4): 94-96.

Holloway, W. H. 1981. A critique of the evaluability assessment model in organizational analysis. A paper prepared for presentation and publication review. ERIC ED 208 565.

Holsti, O. 1969. CONTENT ANALYSIS FOR THE SOCIAL SCIENCES AND HUMANITIES. Reading, MA: Addison-Wesley.

House, E. R. 1980. EVALUATING WITH VALIDITY. Beverly Hills: Sage.

House, E. R. 1986. Drawing evaluative conclusions. EVALUATION PRACTICE, Vol. 7(3): 35-39.

Iker, H. and Klein, R. 1974. WORDS: A computer system for the analysis of content. BEHAVIOR RESEARCH METHODS AND INSTRUMENTATION, Vol. 6: 430-438.

Jones, E. E. 1986. Interpreting interpersonal behavior: The effects of expectancies. SCIENCE, Vol. 234: 41-46.

Jung, S. M. and Schubert, J. G. 1983. Evaluability assessment: A two-year retrospective. EDUCATIONAL EVALUATION AND POLICY ANALYSIS, Vol. 5(4): 435-444.

Kay, P. 1985. Comment made in mini lecture at workshop session on availability assessment at 6th Annual Winter Institute on Evaluating Cooperative Extension Programs. Orlando, Florida: College of Agriculture, University of Florida.

Klein, R. 1982. Evaluation and social policy, some reflections on ideas and institutions. EVALUATION AND PROGRAM PLANNING, Vol. 5: 133-140.

Lawrence, J. E. S. and Cook, T. J. 1982. Designing useful evaluations: The stakeholder survey. EVALUATION AND PROGRAM PLANNING, Vol. 5(4): 327-336.

Lofland, J. 1971. ANALYZING SOCIAL SETTINGS. Belmont, CA: Wadsworth.

MacIntyre, A. 1984. AFTER VIRTUE. Notre Dame: University of Notre Dame Press. In J. K. Smith. 1987. Commentary: Relativism and justifying conclusions in naturalistic evaluations. EVALUATION AND PROGRAM PLANNING, 10(4): 351-358.

Markoff, J., Shapiro, G., and Weitman, S. 1975. Toward the integration of content analysis and general methodology. In D. Heise (ed.), SOCIOLOGICAL METHODOLOGY. San Francisco: Jossey-Bass.

Marshall, C. 1984. The case study evaluation, a means for managing organization and political tensions. EVALUATION AND PROGRAM PLANNING, Vol. 7(3): 253-266.

McClintock, C. 1987. Administrators as information brokers, A managerial perspective on naturalistic evaluation. PROGRAM PLANNING AND EVALUATION 10(4): 315-323.

McCorcle, N. D. 1984. The operation was a success but the patient died: A critique of the implementation and evaluation of a problem-solving training program for adolescents. EVALUATION AND PROGRAM PLANNING, Vol. 7(2): 193-198.

McLuhan, M. 1964. UNDERSTANDING MEDIA. New York: Signet Books.

Mintzberg, H. 1987. Crafting strategy. HARVARD BUSINESS REVIEW. 4: 66-75.

Mitroff, I. I. 1983. STAKEHOLDERS OF THE ORGANIZATIONAL MIND. San Francisco: Jossey-Bass.

Morris, J. N. 1980. Are health services important to the people's health? BRITISH MEDICAL JOURNAL, Vol. 280: 167-168.

Narayanan, A. 1987. THE DEVELOPMENT OF A PROCEDURE FOR ANALYZING QUALITATIVE DATA FROM SEMI-STRUCTURED INTERVIEWS. Masters Thesis, University of Maryland, College Park.

Nay, J. N. and Kay, P. 1982. GOVERNMENT OVERSIGHT AND EVALUABILITY ASSESSMENT. Lexington, MA: Lexington Books.

Nay, J. N. and Kay, P. 1976. EVALUABILITY ASSESSMENT. Washington, D.C.: The Urban Institute. (Working Paper 783-9).

Nay, J., Scanlon, J., and Wholey, J. 1973. Benefits and Costs of Manpower Training Programs: A Synthesis of Previous Studies with Reservations and Recommendations, Paper 80-331. Washington, D.C.: Government Printing Office.

Nelson, P. T. 1987. Evaluability assessment on a shoestring: Delaware's experience with the Family Well-Being plan-of-work. Unpublished study. Newark, DE: Delaware Cooperative Extension.

Nimmo, D. and Combs, J.E. 1983. MEDIATED POLITICAL REALITIES. New York: Longman.

Norris, N. 1981. Problems in the analysis of soft data and some suggested solutions. SOCIOLOGY, Vol. 15(3): 337-351.

Nowakowski, J. 1985. Evaluation for strategy setting. EVALUATION NEWS, Vol. 6(4): 57-61.

Patton, M. Q. 1984. An alternative evaluation approach for the problem-solving training program: A utilization focused evaluation process. EVALUATION AND PROGRAM PLANNING, Vol. 7(2): 189-192.

Patton, M. Q. 1988. Comments after reading a previous iteration of this book. September 12, 1988.

Patton, M. Q. 1983. Similarities of Extension and Evaluation. JOURNAL OF EXTENSION. Vol. 21: 14-21.

Patton, M. Q. 1980. QUALITATIVE EVALUATION. Beverly Hills: Sage.

Pearsol, J. A. 1987. Justifying conclusions in naturalistic evaluations: A practical perspective. EVALUATION AND PROGRAM PLANNING, Vol. 10(4): 335-341.

Petrie, H. G. 1976. Do you see what I see: The epistemology of interdisciplinary inquiry. EDUCATIONAL RESEARCHER, Vol. 5(2): 9-15.

Pittenger, D. and Grieshop, J. 1986. Evaluability Assesment of the Master Gardener Program, University of California, Berkely, CA: California Cooperative Extension.

Rocheleau, B. 1986. Public perception of program effectiveness and worth, a review. EVALUATION AND PROGRAM PLANNING, Vol. 9(1): 31-37.

Rog, D. 1985. A METHODOLOGICAL ANALYSIS OF EVALUABILITY ASSESSMENT. Doctoral Dissertation, Vanderbilt University, Nashville, Tennessee.

Rog, D. J. and Bickman, L. 1984. The feedback research approach to evaluation: A method to increase evaluation utility. EVALUATION AND PROGRAM PLANNING, Vol. 7(2): 169-174.

Rossini, F. A., Porter, A. J., Kelly, P., and Chubin, D. E. 1981. Interdisiplinary integration within technology assessments. KNOWLEDGE: CREATION DIFFUSION UTILIZATION, Vol. 2(4): 503-528.

Russ-Eft, D. 1986. Evaluability assessment of the adult education program (AEP): The results and their uses. EVALUATION AND PROGRAM PLANNING, Vol. 9(1): 39-47.

Rutman, L. 1984. Evaluability assessment. In L. Rutman (ed.), EVALUATION RESEARCH METHODS: A BASIC GUIDE. Beverly Hills: Sage.

Rutman, L. 1986. Evaluation at the federal level. EVALUATION PRACTICE, Vol., 7(2): 14-18.

Rutman, L. (ed.) 1977. EVALUATION RESEARCH METHODS: A BASIC GUIDE. Beverly Hills: Sage.

Rutman, L. 1980. PLANNING USEFUL EVALUATIONS: EVALUABILITY ASSESSMENT. Beverly Hills: Sage.

Rutman, L. and Mowbray, G. 1983. UNDERSTANDING PROGRAM EVALUATION. Beverly Hills: Sage.

Scanlon, J., Buchanan, G., Nay, J., and Wholey, J. 1971. An evaluation system to support planning, allocation, and control in a decentralized, comprehensive manpower program. (Paper 305-3, Washington, D.C. The Urban Institute).

Scanlon, J. W., Horst, P., Nay, J. N., Schmidt, R. E., and Waller, J. D. 1979. Evaluability assessment: Avoiding types III and IV errors. In G. R. Gilbert and P. J. Conklin (eds.), EVALUATION MANAGEMENT: A SELECTION OF READINGS. Washington, D.C.: Office of Personnel Management, Federal Executive Institute.

Scanlon, J., Nay, J., and Wholey, J. 1972. An evaluation system to support a decentralized, comprehensive manpower program. In M. E. Borus (ed.) EVALUATING THE IMPACT OF MANPOWER PROGRAMS. Lexington, MA: D.C. Heath and Company.

Scheerens, J. 1987. Beyond decision-oriented evaluation. INTERNATIONAL JOURNAL OF EDUCATIONAL RESEARCH. Vol. 2(1): 105-114.

Scheirer, M. A. 1987. Program theory & implementation theory: implications for evaluators. In L. Bickman (ed.) USING PROGRAM THEORY IN EVALUATION. New Directions for Program Evaluation, No. 33. San Francisco: Jossey-Bass.

Schmidt, R. E., Scanlon, J. W., and Bell, J. B. 1979. Evaluability assessment: Making public programs work better. HUMAN SERVICES MONOGRAPH SERIES, No. 14.

Schubert, J. G. 1982. Evaluability assessment: The promise in practice. Paper presented at the Annual Meeting of the American Educational Research Association. (New York, NY, March 19-23).

Scriven, M. 1967. The methodology of evaluation. In R. W. Tyler, R. M. Gagne, and M. Scriven (eds.), PERSPECTIVES OF CURRICULUM EVALUATION. AERA Monograph Series on Curriculum Evaluation, No. 1. Chicago: Rand McNally.

Scriven, M. 1985. New frontiers of evaluation. EVALUATION PRACTICE, Vol. 7(1): 7-44.

Shadish, W. R., Jr. 1987. Program micro- and macrotheories: A guide for social change. In L. Bickman (ed.), USING PROGRAM THEORY IN EVALUATION. New Directions for Program Evaluation, No. 33. San Francisco: Jossey-Bass.

Sherrill, S. 1974. Identifying and measuring unintended outcomes. EVALUATION AND PROGRAM PLANNING, Vol. 7(1): 27-34.

Smith, J. K. 1987. Commentary: Relativism and justifying conclusions in naturalistic evaluations. EVALUATION AND PROGRAM PLANNING, Vol. 10(4) 351-358.

Smith, M. F. 1988. Evaluation utilization revisited. NEW DIRECTIONS FOR PROGRAM EVALUATION, Vol. 39: 7-19.

Smith, M. F. 1983. SAMPLING CONSIDERATIONS IN EVALUATING COOPERATIVE EXTENSION PROGRAMS, PE-1. Gainesville, FL: Institute of Food and Agricultural Sciences, University of Florida.

Smith, M. F. and Lincoln, Y. S. 1984. Another kind of evaluation. JOURNAL OF EXTENSION, Vol. 22: 5-10.

Smith, M. F. and Straughn, A. A. 1983. Impact evaluation: A challenge for Extension. JOURNAL OF EXTENSION, Vol. 21: 55-63.

Smith, N. L. 1987. Toward the justification of claims in evaluation research. EVALUATION AND PROGRAM PLANNING, Vol. 10(4): 309-314.

Smith, V. L. 1986. Experimental methods in the political economy of exchange. SCIENCE, Vol. 234: 167-173.

Smithson, M. 1981. A method for evaluating and improving goal consensus for social action programs. EVALUATION AND PROGRAM PLANNING, Vol. 4(3-4): 261-271.

Sprott, J. M. 1977. STATEMENT PREPARED FOR U.S. HOUSE OF REPRESENTATIVES, COMMITTEE ON AGRICULTURE, SUBCOMMITTEE ON FORESTS, RESOURCE PLANNING ACT (RPA) OVERSIGHT HEARING. (October 18.) Washington, D.C.

Suchman, E. A. 1967. EVALUATION RESEARCH: PRINCIPLES AND PRACTICE IN PUBLIC SERVICE AND SOCIAL ACTION PROGRAMS. New York: Russell Sage.

Sudman, S. 1976. APPLIED SAMPLING. New York: Academic Press.

Summerhill, W. R. 1983. Considerations in questionnaire design. Paper at Fourth Annual Winter Institute on Evaluation of Cooperative Extension Programs. Gainesville, FL: Institute of Food and Agricultural Sciences, University of Florida.

Taylor, J. B. 1975. Building an interdisciplinary team. In S. Arnstein and A Christakis (eds.), PERSPECTIVES ON TECHNOLOGY ASSESSMENT. Jerusalem: Science and Technology Publishers.

Tornatzky, L. G. and Johnson, E. C. 1982. Research on implementation, implications for evaluation practice and evaluation policy. EVALUATION AND PROGRAM PLANNING, Vol. 5(3): 193-198.

Vogt, L., White, T., Bucanan, G., Wholey, J., and Zamoff, R. 1973. HEALTH START: FINAL REPORT OF THE EVALUATION OF THE SECOND YEAR PROGRAM. Washington, D. C.: The Urban Institute.

Webb, E. J., Campbell, D.T., Schwartz, R.D., and L. Sechrest. 1966. UNOBTRUSIVE MEASURES. Chicago: Rand McNally.

Weiss, C.H. 1973. Between the cup and the lip. EVALUATION, Vol. 1(2): 49-55.

Weiss, C. H. 1975. Interviewing in evaluation research. In E. L. Struening and M. Brewer (eds.), HANDBOOK OF EVALUATION RESEARCH, Vol. 1. Beverly Hills: Sage.

White, B., Kelley, S., MacNeil, D., Nay, J., Waller, J., and Wholey, J. 1974. THE ATLANTA PROJECT: HOW ONE LARGE SCHOOL SYSTEM RESPONDED TO PERFORMANCE INFORMATION. Washington, D. C.: The Urban Institute.

Wholey, J. S. 1987. Evaluability assessment: Developing program theory. In L. Bickman (ed.), USING PROGRAM THEORY IN EVALUATION. New Directions for Program Evaluation, No. 33. San Francisco: Jossey-Bass.

Wholey, J. S. 1983. EVALUATION AND EFFECTIVE PUBLIC MANAGEMENT. Boston: Little, Brown & Co.

Wholey, J. S. 1979. EVALUATION: PROMISE AND PERFORMANCE. Washington, D. S.: The Urban Institute.

Wholey, J. S. 1986. Using evaluation to improve government program performance. EVALUATION PRACTICE, Vol. 7(2): 5-13.

Wholey, J. S. 1981. Using evaluation to improve performance. In H. E. Freedman and M. A. Solomon (eds.), EVALUATION STUDIES REVIEW ANNUAL, Vol. 6: 55-69.

Wholey, J. S., Abramson, M. S., and Bellavita, C. (eds.) 1986. PERFORMANCE AND CREDIBILITY: DEVELOPING EXCELLENCE IN PUBLIC AND NONPROFIT ORGANIZATIONS. Lexington, MA.: D. C. Heath & Co.

Williams, W. 1976. Implementation analysis and assessment. In W. Williams and R. F. Elmore (eds.) 1976. SOCIAL PROGRAM IMPLEMENTATION. New York: Academic Press.

Williams, W. and Elmore, R. F. (eds.) 1976. SOCIAL PROGRAM IMPLEMENTATION. New York: Academic Press.

Woodram, E. 1984 Mainstreaming content analysis in social science: Methodological advantages, obstacles, and solutions. SOCIAL SCIENCE RESEARCH, Vol. 13: 1-19.

Index